My Stroke
of Luck

Also by Kirk Douglas

wm

William Morrow

An Imprint of HarperCollins*Publishers*

My
Stroke
of
Luck

Kirk
Douglas

Photograph on page 50 by Brewster Thackery for the
National Organization on Disability. Photograph on page 55
by Don Flood. All other photographs courtesy of the
author's collection.

HarperCollins books may be purchased for educational,
business, or sales promotional use. For information please write:
Special Markets Department, HarperCollins Publishers Inc.,
10 East 53rd Street, New York, NY 10022.

FIRST EDITION

Designed by Gretchen Achilles

Printed on acid-free paper

Library of Congress Cataloging-in-Publication Data has been
applied for.

ISBN 0-06-000929-2

02   03   04   05   06   QW   10   9   8   7   6   5   4   3   2   1

Sometimes, I feel like a cowboy, slowly riding my horse, Whiskey, into the sunset. As I lope along, I think of my life; after a stroke, I made two films with impaired speech. Now I am waiting for another part to play before the sun sinks below the horizon. You can't stop an actor. Like the Energizer bunny, "he keeps going, and going, and going. . . ."

I have been so lucky to be an actor! It has given me fame, money, and satisfaction. Still, I discouraged my sons from entering my profession. The chances of success are so remote; the pitfalls of failure and depression lie hidden along the trail. Alas, they don't listen to me.

"Whoa, Whiskey." I dismount and sit in the shade of a stately oak tree and stare off, hypnotized by the sheer brilliance of the setting sun. Whiskey is chomping on grass, oblivious to the yellow orb that lights up the sky. It burns brightly and then fades. I shudder, but there is no breeze.

My thoughts turn to a long time past. I think of Burt Lancaster, Duke Wayne, and the many actors I have been honored to work with in my life. I think of all those I never had that privilege to work with, actors I admired from afar.

We are entertainers. We make films to give people a short respite from the problems in their lives as they are swept up in the make-believe world on the screen. But actors live in the real world, too. And we have our own woes.

I admire my colleagues who show courage in the face of personal tragedy instead of crawling away in self-pity. I applaud loudly Christopher Reeve, Michael J. Fox, Dudley Moore, and so many others who use their celebrity to bring light to the darkness. To help others is the will of God.

To them, I dedicate this book.

The sun has set. In the twilight, Whiskey and I ride back to see if my agent has called.

Acknowledgments

A computer is a good help when you are writing a book, but I don't know how to use one. Thankfully, my assistant, Lisa Lynn, does. She was able to take my dictation directly and type it all into the computer. What a help that was! Thank you, Lisa.

Very often, I needed a sounding board— someone to agree or disagree with my point of

Acknowledgments

view. Eliana Wolpe played that role. Her intelligent comments were a big help. Thank you, Elli.

Of course, my publishing editor, Claire Wachtel, was of great assistance. Her staff convinced me that I am not a grammarian—and I thank them for their valuable suggestions.

If it takes a village to raise a child, then it certainly takes more than one person to write a book. Except if that one person is my wife, Anne.

I thank them all.

One.

How It Happened

It was a sunny afternoon (not unusual in Los Angeles). I was in my room, lounging in a chair, having a manicure (ah, the lifestyles of the rich and famous). My wife, Anne, insists that I have a regular manicure. She cannot bear the sight of my peasant hands if they are not properly manicured.

I like this room. I do all my work here—writing,

studying scripts, reading a book, watching television, and dreaming. I gave up my office long ago. This is where I exist. I turn the phone off—that shrill siren song of the outside world. The only constant visitors to my lair are my dogs, Danny and Foxy, both Labradors. I couldn't pet them now because my hands were being beautified.

I was feeling pretty good since the surgery on my back, ready to make a golf date, dreaming about hitting a long drive on the fourth hole. Suddenly, I felt a peculiar sensation in my right cheek.

It was as if a pointed object had drawn a line from my temple, made a half circle on my cheek, and stopped. I felt no pain, but when I tried to describe it to Rose, my manicurist, I couldn't talk. What came out was gibberish. What was happening to me? Rose had been a nurse in Israel and knew immediately that I was having a stroke. She ran to the kitchen to ask Concha, our cook, to call

Anne, who was at that moment playing bridge with Barbara Sinatra.

An alarmed Concha rushed into the room and began slapping my face, intoning Mexican prayers. I tried to tell her that slapping was not helping me. But all that came out of my mouth was babble. She kept slapping. I was bewildered.

Anne hurried home and got on the phone to my doctor. Dr. Rick Gold told her, "If he can move, drive him to the hospital—an ambulance would take too long."

I looked at Anne. There was fear in her eyes, but she tried to reassure me in a matter-of-fact way. I did not try to speak. My mind was in turmoil. I still did not know what had happened to me. Now everybody was being very calm, too calm. It bothered me. Before being led to the car, I looked at my hands. I turned to Rose: "Hey, you didn't finish my nails." My joke fell flat—no one understood me.

When we arrived at a private entrance, two doctors were waiting at the end of a long hall. They were relieved to see me walk. This indicated that I had no paralysis in my legs.

Dr. Gold asked, "Show me your teeth." I bared my teeth as I have done in so many of my movies. What I did not know was that my right lip drooped down, covering my teeth at that side of my mouth. It was a sure sign of stroke. I could understand everything the doctor said, but I could not talk.

They quickly sent me for a CAT scan. A CAT scan uses X rays; an MRI, which uses magnetic resonance, was out of the question because of my pacemaker, inserted into my chest six years earlier. (But that's another story.) When they slid me into that enclosed channel, I was frightened. "What's happening to me?" The beating of my heart seemed louder than the mechanical buzz of the machine taking pictures of my brain. I shut my eyes in the darkness.

My Stroke of Luck

"Am I going to die?" I just recovered from an operation on my back!

They rolled me back into the light. I preferred the darkness. I wanted to obliterate everything. They tried to calm me down: "With exercise and speech therapy, you will regain your speech." They put me on a gurney, assuring me, "It's just a minor stroke."

What the hell are they talking about? A stroke! I just came out of this same hospital a month ago, after enduring an operation on my back from my helicopter crash. Strokes are for elderly people, with slurred speech, moving about in walkers or wheelchairs. I was only eighty; how can a stroke happen to me? Does that mean there will be no golf tomorrow?

Later, I learned that I had suffered a brain attack. That's what strokes really are. Brain attacks are the third leading cause of death in America. Every minute someone in the United

States has a stroke. That means more than 700,000 people each year. While you read this page, two more people will have a stroke. Thirty percent of those who suffer strokes are under the age of sixty-five. What chance do I have, I'm nearly twenty years older?

As I was wheeled down the hospital corridor, I looked up at the ceiling lights passing over me. Didn't I see this scene in a movie? The doctor's words echoed in my mind: It's just a minor stroke.

Yeah, minor to you, major to me. I was frightened.

In my hospital room, Dr. Gold, our regular internist, tried to lessen my fears. "Kirk, you did a picture with Janet Leigh."

"*The Vikings,*" I muttered.

"Tell me." And he leaned closer to me. "Are those big boobs real?"

"What?" I couldn't believe it!

"Are those beautiful boobs real?"

" 'Course!"

"How do you know, did you ever touch them? Did you see them?"

I shook my head in exasperation. "Real!"

"Boy, I always had a crush on her."

And so the conversation continued. I never told Janet that the doctor used the image of her breasts to take my mind off my problems.

For twenty hours, I was forbidden to eat or drink until the doctors were convinced that my esophagus was not impaired and that I could swallow. Finally, they gave me something to drink and watched me intensely. They did not want me to choke to death. That thought sent shivers through my body. Death! Yesterday I was ready to play golf. Now what?

Two.
Death Takes
a Holiday

I recall five incidents in my life when I came close to death. More than seventy-five years ago, as a boy of five, I nearly drowned.

Next to our house, a five-foot trench had been dug to lay the foundation for another mill. A water pipe burst, and the trench filled up with water. It was Sunday, and no workers were around. My playmates and I were using the area as a playground.

I must have been a dumb kid, because I placed a pole across the ditch filled with water and tried to walk to the other side. Needless to say, I slipped in, and wouldn't you know it, I couldn't swim. As I was thrashing around, yelling for help, I saw my two young classmates running home because they were frightened. But suddenly I was being pulled from the water by an older schoolmate, Wolfie. I ran home, crying. Pa spanked me for getting my clothes wet.

Then there were close calls while I was at work. In 1954, I was making *The Indian Fighter*. I was working with Walter Matthau, who had just come from the Broadway stage. We were standing near the top of the fort, shooting blanks at the Indians. The stuntmen, playing Indians, were shooting arrows, fitted with five-inch steel tips so they would be sure to stick into the wood of the fort. One came whistling three inches from my head and embedded itself deep in a wood post that I was leaning against. A few inches closer and . . . well, I'm not quite sure what happens if a five-inch piece of steel enters your head, but it can't be good.

In Spain in the fall of 1971, I was shooting a movie with Yul Brynner called *Light at the Edge of the World*. The scene called for a fight on a roof. I fell off and cracked my head against a rock. I was in a coma for five days.

The next incident started in New York in 1989. After dinner, Anne and I joined Frank Sinatra at Jimmy's, a nightclub. I knew Frank for fifty years. He was a charismatic character, a heavy drinker and a heavy smoker. But it never seemed to affect that glorious voice. The episodes with Frank could fill another book. But the most devastating memory I have is of the time when he became fatally ill. I had a quick glimpse of Frank in his wheelchair before he was pushed out of sight. Anne and I would go over to play poker with Barbara (Frank was always in his room), usually with Jack Lemmon, Greg Peck, Larry Gelbart, and their wives. Joking around the table, I couldn't help but wonder, what was Frank, sitting in his wheelchair, thinking? Did he remember the girls screaming his name outside of the Paramount Theater sixty years ago? I remember, I was trying to work my way through the crowd to get to the Forty-second Street subway station. Here now was Frank, in his cocoon. He never came out of it. It was hard to imagine someone overflowing with vitality and talent rendered so helpless. Could it happen to me? But I'm getting away from my story of the night at Jimmy's nightclub. Barbara Sinatra, the smart one, went to bed. I was dancing with Anne, when suddenly I became dizzy and could not stand. They had to help me off the dance floor. Frank chided me for not being able to hold my liquor. Anne was not so sure.

Weeks later, we had just arrived at Chasen's to have dinner with friends. As I reached over to kiss the cheek of our dinner partner, I became dizzy and fell to the floor. I was carried out to the lobby and laid down on the sofa. A doctor, who happened to be dining there, took my pulse. He whispered to Anne, "Very low." Then he turned to me and said softly, "Don't be frightened." I muttered, "Take me home." My wife wisely ignored my request and called for an ambulance. On the drive to Cedars-Sinai Hospital, the paramedics gave my heart two injections. Later, after my pacemaker was safely tucked inside my chest, the doctor said, "If your wife had taken you home, you would have died." Great.

Then, in 1991, just two years later, I survived a helicopter crash. Fifty feet in the air, we smashed into a small plane that was just taking off. The plane exploded and two occupants were

With Frank Sinatra cooking dinner for Anne's birthday.

killed instantly. We crashed to the tarmac and I was rushed to the hospital, suffering a compressed spine. Lying in bed, I learned that these two victims on the plane were very young. One, eighteen, was planning to go to his senior prom that week. The other, a young instructor, was scheduled to give a talk that night on safety in the air. I was in my seventies. I felt very guilty. I wrote to the families of both of them; an inadequate note I'm sure. I visited the father of the high-school student. I met him at the same airport where the collision had occurred. In a corner were the remains of the helicopter, a pile of crushed metal. He was with his other son, a tall, handsome boy. I never felt so inadequate. The father just looked at me with a faint smile. I felt very guilty. What could I say to make him feel better about the death of his young son? I felt like a criminal for being alive.

Dr. Goldstein, a back specialist, took an X ray of my back after the crash. In my room, looking at the film, he said, "Kirk, did you do your own stunts in movies?"

"I tried to," I said.

"I can see that." (Still looking at the film.) "This is the worst back I have ever seen. I would hate to operate—I wouldn't know where to start." Progressively, my injury led to more severe back pain. For months, I spent most of my time lying on the floor feeling sorry for myself. If I tried to sit, I howled about the pain in my back. After a few years of unbearable pain, Dr. Goldstein had to operate. He worked a miracle—the pain in my back subsided. I quickly graduated from a wheelchair to a cane, and finally, "Look, Ma, I can walk."

I have often wondered, if any of those incidents had delivered me to death's door, would I have had the courage to smile and quote my mother: "Don't be afraid, it happens to everyone"?

In 1952, when I was only forty-two, my mother was dying. I held her frail hand in mine for hours, looking at the pale face of my ma. That's what I always called her—not Mum, not Momma, not Mother—just Ma. This woman, an illiterate immigrant from Russia, had come to America to meet her husband, my father, who had made the journey two years before.

What a hard life she endured. I kept studying her face. My mother's eyes opened and she stared at my face, filled with anxiety. She smiled softly and squeezed my hand gently. Her eyes, almost black on her white face, seemed to be looking through me. She whispered, "Don't be afraid, it happens to everyone." She took a deep breath and exhaled. The air came out of her mouth like a slowly deflating balloon. She stopped breathing.

Her startling last words still echo somewhere deep inside of me. My mother, in her last moments, was concerned about me. She was a real mother who took care of me till the very end of her life.

Now, lying in my hospital bed, I wondered: What happens when you die? Could I see my mother again? I would like that.

But maybe, after death, you come before that mythical Man with a long beard, sitting on a throne. You stand before Him, puny and timid. Then you ask, "Is this heaven?" And He roars back, "HEAVEN! You just came from there!"

And as your eyes widen, He continues, "Ingrate! Didn't you like the sunrise, the sunset, the moon, and the stars? Weren't you pleased with the mountains, forests, rivers, and streams that I gave you?" I remain silent as the voice roars. "Didn't you like the fragrant flowers and fruits and vegetables I gave you? And when I nurtured those plants with rain, you complained because you couldn't play golf. Ingrate! That was heaven!"

And then I dare to ask, "Well, what is this

place?" He laughs: "This is the recycling plant. Here, you turn back to dust." I stand there and stare at Him. "Don't you understand? DUST THOU ART, AND TO DUST THOU SHALT RETURN."

He didn't have to bellow.

Three.
Inventory

A hospital bed was installed in my room at home, and it soon became my cocoon. I didn't feel frightened there. I looked around the room. This is where it all happened. The chair I sat in at my desk. The Bible series of Chagall were on the wall. They comfort me. Straight ahead is my bookcase, filled with books that I had read, all signed by the authors. On the top shelf is a row of scripts of every movie I had done, each one bound in black leather. More than eighty of them. How many thousands of words would that add up to? I said all of those words at one time with ease. Now how many words will I be able to utter? I am an eighty-year-old man with a stroke. I'm an actor, and I can't talk. Is this THE END? Maybe I could study with Marcel Marceau and become a mime, but that thought didn't make me laugh. I was tired of being a big, strong, tough guy. I began to cry. The room seemed to get darker and a big black cloud engulfed me. I cried and cried until my pillow became wet with my tears. Both dogs perked up their ears and watched me. They seemed to have sympathy in their eyes. They jumped up on the bed. Danny was licking my face, while Foxy lay very still. But I didn't want to see anybody. I didn't want anybody to see me. What good is an actor who can't talk?

I lay like that, in the darkness, almost comatose, my head stuffed in the pillow for a long time. Sometimes, my wife, sons, friends, came in to see me, but I didn't see them. I didn't hear them. Sometimes, I didn't know whether it was day or night. It seemed as if I was in a black cave far down below the surface of the earth. With eyes closed, I just lay there, constantly swallowing the saliva leaking out of my mouth. I wiped my chin with the sheet.

I had read about people suffering from depression: I had scoffed at it. Stop whining and take an aspirin. I was a fool. Here I was, curled up in a bundle of fear, feeling so sorry for myself. I felt so helpless—so useless. I will never make another movie—I will never write another book. Will I ever talk again? Everything seemed hopeless, hopeless. Each day I did nothing but lie in this black hole, which only seemed to get smaller and darker.

With an effort, I pulled myself out of bed and

stumbled to the bathroom. I dared to look in the mirror. My face was covered with a scraggly, white stubble. My tongue was thick. I couldn't swallow my saliva fast enough; it was constantly dripping out of the corner of my mouth, drooping on the right side. My face was grotesque. I could not stop crying. I felt such deep shame and disgust. I hated myself.

I walked over to the desk. In the lower drawer is the gun I used in *Gunfight at the O.K. Corral,* a film I made with Burt Lancaster. I picked it up. We had some pretty good times together. I smiled as I conjured up a vision of Burt introducing me at an award function. "Kirk Douglas would be the first to admit he is a very difficult person. And I would be the second."

Our last film was *Tough Guys.* I put the gun down. We weren't so tough. I remember when we were rehearsing a play, *The Boys in Autumn.* Burt was very anxious to do the play. Much more than I was. It was based on the characters of Tom Sawyer and Huckleberry Finn, fifty years later in their lives. At the rehearsal, we got into an argument (we often did). I decided not to do the play and walked off. Burt ran and grabbed me. I was stunned. Tears were rolling down his cheeks. He implored me not to back out. We did the play for six weeks in San Francisco. No, we weren't so tough.

Suddenly, while visiting a friend in the hospital, Burt crumbled to the floor with a stroke. He lived four years as a speechless invalid. What were his thoughts, sitting in his wheelchair, helpless? Was he thinking of the days we galloped across the desert together? Did he ever reminisce about the song-and-dance routines we did at the Oscars—"It's great not to be nominated!" Or our big hit at the Palladium in London—"Maybe it's because I'm a Londoner that I love London so!" We were so athletic then. I climbed up on his shoulders and doffed my bowler, and we sang the finish and went into a somersault.

Kirk Douglas

With Burt Lancaster in the play The Boys in Autumn *in San Francisco. We were a hit!*

I didn't have a chance to say good-bye to Burt. That made me cry. His wife would not permit me to see him, fearing it would depress him. But people who saw him were not sure they were recognized. If he could, wouldn't he prefer to end that embarrassing state? No, I'm not going to wait for that.

Again, I picked up the gun. In another drawer, I had a box of bullets. I took out two of them, and with the other hand flipped open the chamber of the gun. I loaded the gun and looked at it. In my mouth or at the temple?

I stuck the long barrel of the gun in my mouth and it bumped against my teeth. "Ow!" It sent shivers through my teeth, and I pulled the gun out.

I began to laugh. A toothache delayed my death. I laughed hysterically. I felt like I was playing a part in a movie. "Too many movies, too many movies." I kept laughing. Fifi, our housekeeper, knocked at the door. "Are you okay, Mr. D.?" "Yes, Fifi, it's okay." But I couldn't stop laughing. Fifi appeared at the door and looked at me. The last time she saw me, a few hours earlier, I was a morose invalid in bed. By the way, Fifi is much more than a housekeeper. After thirty-nine years, she is part of the family. For example, one day I was looking in my closet for my favorite slacks. "Fifi," I called out, "where're the slacks that I always wear?"

Her answer: "I threw them out!"

"What? Why?"

"You can't wear slacks like that! They're too old." She left me stuttering.

Humor saved me that day in my room with the gun. Suicide! What a selfish act. I thought about the people I would leave behind to grieve. My wife, my sons, maybe a friend or two. And what a mess for Fifi to clean up! I put the gun away.

I quickly went back to my cocoon with a guilty feeling. I once again pulled the covers over me. Here, I felt safe. Outside lurked danger.

My Stroke of Luck

There must be thousands of stroke victims right now who have given up. Some write to me. They don't go out of the house. They don't try to communicate. They have forgotten how to laugh. They just do nothing and wait . . . for what?

Four.

Sleep, Sleep,
the Innocent Sleep

I had lots of time to think, lying there staring up at the ceiling, day after day, night after night. The doctors hesitated to give me more medication, but I found a way to solve that problem. During the day I searched my mind for some thought that I could enjoy before going to sleep. When I found a good memory, like a dog I hid my favorite bone, to be chewed on later. At night, I rearranged the pillows to make myself comfortable and allowed my imagination to go back almost seventy-five years.

I am six years old, all alone in the kitchen with my mother. It is winter. The fire is crackling in the stove. My mother is humming a song while stirring a pot. Best of all, my sisters are in school, and the baby is sleeping. I am happy; I have my mother to myself. I look out the window. It is snowing.

"Ma, where does the snow come from?"

My mother never stops stirring. "That's the angels sweeping the porch of heaven."

Gee, I think to myself, heaven must be a clean place—angels sweeping snow that falls silently on the cold earth. In the house it is warm. I watch my mother put another piece of wood in the stove. The fire is crackling—we are alone, and I am happy. I dread the time when my six sisters come home.

"Ma, how was I born?"

My mother looks over her shoulder, still tossing onions into the pot.

"Well, how was I born, Ma?"

Ma wipes her hands on her apron, comes over, and puts her arms around me. "It was a morning just like this." And she points out the window. "Snowing, cold."

She hesitates, but I urge her on: "And then what?"

"I was cooking lunch for your sisters, who were in school." My mother rises and walks to the sink and starts scrubbing potatoes.

"And then what?" I push.

"Well, I heard a noise outside. I rubbed the frost off the window and looked out. I was so surprised." She is still scrubbing.

"What did you see, what did you see?"

With a sigh, Ma comes back, puts her arms around me again, and gives me a squeeze. "I saw a gold box, two feet above the ground, held at each corner by four silver strings going up to the sky."

"Wow! What did you do?"

"I grabbed a shawl and ran out. It was a shiny gold box, carved with flowers, and the silver strings were glistening."

"Did you open it? Did you open it?" I hold my breath with excitement.

And she nods.

"What was in it?"

Ma turns to me with a big smile. "You."

"ME?!"

"Yes, naked and red. I wrapped you up in the shawl, quickly took you into the house to warm you by the stove."

So that was how I was born. I am stunned.

"And what happened to the gold box? Where is it?"

My mother takes my face in her two hands and looks at me. "I was so happy to find you that I didn't even think about the box, and later, when I looked out, it was gone."

"Gee, Ma, you should have—"

Just then my sisters stumble into the house, stomping their shoes to remove the snow and all talking at once. I am angry. It was so peaceful without them. I wanted to ask more questions.

And then I fell asleep, curled up in a gold box.

When I ran out of pleasant moments with my mother, I tried to find one pleasant memory with my father—Pa, who never gave me a pat on the back. I searched and searched in my past to find one. Just one memory with my father that would quiet my fears in the dark of night, as I lay in my bed. I couldn't find a single one. I gave up.

One day, while I was working with my speech therapist, she suggested that I use ice to stimulate

Kirk Douglas

Pa, who never gave me a pat on the back; Ma, who never stopped patting.

the tissue in my lips and tongue. She added that I could even use some ice cream. Ice cream!

Eureka! I found that moment. All day I gathered that memory of ice cream and my father.

That night, I quickly curled up in bed, closed my eyes, and let my thoughts wander.

I saw the curtain of my school stage open. There I was—eight years old, dressed in a black apron that Ma made for me. I was playing the role of a shoe- maker, singing a song as he works on a shoe. "I'm Tack Hammer, the shoemaker."

Sophie, a plump girl of seven, was playing my wife, busily cooking dinner on a stove, fired by a burning lightbulb. I had too much work to do. But when my wife and I slept, elves appeared and did much of the work.

This was my first time on a stage. The audience loved the little thespians, and applauded gener- ously.

Unbeknownst to me, my father had come into the school and stood in the back of the room and

With my six sisters, three older, three younger: Kay, Ruth, Fritzie, Ida, Marion, and Betty.

watched the play. I was so surprised to find Pa at the end of the show. He never revealed any interest in my activities as a child.

This time, he took my little hand in his big, callused mitt and bought me an ice-cream cone. What joy, as he walked me home, one hand holding his, the other stuffing ice cream in my mouth!

Five.

Depression:
Woe Is Me

I sit here at my desk writing—or should I say scribbling? A stroke doesn't improve your handwriting. Fifi, our housekeeper, comes into the room. Without a word, she places a beautiful vase of flowers in front of me. Roses, just picked from the garden beyond my window. Usually I enjoy looking at these voluptuous flowers, with their overwhelming fragrance. Now, in the midst of my depression, these flowers were always there, but I could not see them.

I seemed to be wearing blinders. In my narrow vision, I was deeply immersed in what was the essence of my depression: self-pity. It was devastating.

Of course there was anger and despair, and especially fear. But those feelings concerned only me, without any thought of the outside world. I was saturated in thoughts of woe: how could this happen to me? My wife and sons did all they could to help me cope, but I wasn't listening. It never occurred to me to think of other people's problems.

At least I was in fashion. Depression is being talked about as almost a "designer disease," with new medications on the market guaranteed to change the dark shadows back to rose-colored hues. Scientists are studying what brings it on: a state of helplessness, low self-esteem, no desire to live, post-traumatic stress, an indefinable inner pain.

My dogs, Danny and Foxy, spent a lot of time in my room, lying on the floor or curled up with me in bed. One day, I heard Foxy moaning and whining. I opened my eyes and saw him standing in front of the door, looking pleadingly at me. I got up, opened the door, and he left wagging his tail.

I was stunned. It was an epiphany. My dogs, who are always there to help me, also needed help. People need help. And I lie in bed, accepting or ignoring the help they give me. I found the one thing that took me out of myself, out of my sadness, out of my fear, and out of my darkness: helping others. It gave me hope and courage.

While studying religion with Rabbi Wolpe, I remembered the story of the Lubavitcher rabbi of Chabad, who also suffered a stroke before he died. He said depression has to do with the anguish of

Kirk Douglas

My two loyal friends, Foxy and Danny.

the soul. He wrote: "Have you ever just burst out in tears for no apparent reason, finding yourself in deep sadness? That is the soft voice of your soul, crying out for attention, asking to be nourished with at least as much care as you nourish your body."

The world is filled with people who have suffered from one misfortune or another. The only thing that sets one apart from the rest is the desire and the attempt to help others. People who reach out beyond their pain, out into the world in a trusting way—they are the ones who make a difference. Nietzsche said, "He who has a *why* to live for can bear with almost any *how*."

Six.

Presidents

I admire Ronald Reagan. He had the courage to write a letter to the world when he knew he had Alzheimer's disease. This courageous act, speaking so openly about a disease that would inevitably conquer him, helped so many other people, not only those with that treacherous malady, but also their friends and family.

In 1997, a year after my stroke, I established a

unit for Alzheimer's disease in the Motion Picture Home. I called it Harry's Haven, after my father, although he never had Alzheimer's.

My friends thought that Harry's Haven sounded like a saloon, but that was all right with me. Pa spent a lot of time in saloons.

I established this place not so much for the people afflicted with that terrible disease, but for their families. Can you imagine living every day with a loved one who doesn't know who you are? He can't share any memories with you of the past, and has no awareness of the present or future.

Anne often has lunch with Mrs. Reagan. I got glimpses of the life she has had to bear.

But the president who did the most, in adversity, for the handicapped was Franklin Delano Roosevelt. FDR was our only president who held office for three consecutive terms. He served during the most tumultuous times in our history—the aftermath of the Depression, World War II, the

With my family at the opening of the Alzheimer's unit, which I called Harry's Haven in honor of my father.

development of the atom bomb—and he still had the energy to deal with national problems. He did all this from a wheelchair.

In his youth, Roosevelt was a very active athlete, engaged in playing polo, tennis, hunting, and swimming. In 1921, he was stricken with infantile paralysis. The muscles of his legs were paralyzed. From that time until his death (he died suddenly from cerebral hemorrhage—i.e., a stroke), he had to use a wheelchair. When he had to make a speech, he stood up with hidden braces. He designed a contraption for himself out of a kitchen chair mounted on tricycle wheels. Many people never knew because they never saw him in the wheelchair. This could never happen today. The media was more considerate then, and never took pictures showing his disability.

Many people felt that the secrecy about FDR's paralysis did a disservice to the handicapped. They wanted to remedy that. Fifty-five years after his death, the famous sculptor Robert Graham was engaged to make a statue of the president in his wheelchair. Of course there was a huge response— pro and con—but Graham completed the statue of the president in his homemade wheelchair, with an upturned face, but without the usual cigarette. This bronze likeness of a defiant Franklin Delano Roosevelt was unveiled at the FDR Memorial. Graham created a work of art that inspired the nation, especially the handicapped. Disabled groups poured into this memorial near the Potomac River to see the man who did it all from his wheelchair.

President Clinton, who attended the unveiling, said he especially liked that the statue was low enough for those in wheelchairs to touch, and touch it they did. When President Clinton dedicated the statue, he called Roosevelt an "incredibly brave man whose disability made him more free for his spirit to soar and his nation to survive and prosper."

Hannah McFadden, an Albanian immigrant who was born with a leg deformity, said it best as she touched the statue: "It means people on crutches and in a wheelchair can do anything!"

On a wall, behind the new figure of FDR, are inscribed the words of his wife, Eleanor: "Franklin's illness . . . gave him the strength and

Kirk Douglas

From a wheelchair, FDR was elected three times as our president—and the world listened to him.

courage he had not had before . . . and infinite patience and never-ending persistence."

Congressman Jim Langevin of Rhode Island, the first quadriplegic elected to Congress, said at the unveiling, "This is a shrine for people who in some way or another have overcome challenges in their lives."

Ah, how much I owe these people—much stronger than I. Thinking of their achievements has helped me so much. Sometimes God gives us obstacles in life to overcome to make us stronger.

Seven.

Little Heroes

I am inspired by the courage of so many prominent people who openly confront their handicaps to help others. I am proud that so many are in my profession.

Mike Wallace suffered from depression for years. He became suicidal. Diagnosis: depression of unknown origin. Bravely, he openly discussed his illness on national TV in an attempt to help others.

Tipper Gore, wife of the former vice president Al Gore, has also discussed her bouts with depression. I admire this attractive woman with courage. She dared to speak openly about her problems in order to help other people.

Then there is the wonderful Christopher Reeve, in his wheelchair, sharing words of encouragement with others, investing all of his energy and efforts to find a way to reverse the damage done to people with spinal cord injuries. Reeve, with difficulty, speaks out optimistically in his campaign to find a cure.

I look with pride at my friend Michael J. Fox. We did a movie together, *Greedy,* a few years ago. He has such vitality, humor. We had fun working together. Now he is battling Parkinson's disease, but he is not wallowing in self-pity. He's helping others.

Christopher Reeve, a real hero, who has dedicated his life to helping others.

I remember, years ago, in 1949, I escorted Patricia Neal to the premiere of *The Fountain-*

head, a movie she made with Gary Cooper. I brought her home and kissed her good night, passionately, as I remember, and often. A jealous Gary Cooper was watching from across the street. When I discovered this, it embarrassed me. I had great admiration for Gary Cooper. Did I interfere with their relationship? I felt guilty about that for a long time. He was in love with her, but he was married.

I liked Patricia very much. She was young, beautiful, and strong. She got over Gary Cooper, whose wife would never divorce him, and married a writer, Roald Dahl. Who could anticipate the tragedy that followed? Patricia had not one, but three near-fatal strokes. I visited her. Gone was the vital person with the throaty laugh: She was so broken. How awful, I thought, to have a stroke. But Patricia never gave up, and in five years she

With my friend Michael J. Fox, when we worked together in Greedy.

had overcome these tragedies and started working again.

Stephen Hawking is regarded as the most brilliant theoretical physicist since Albert Einstein. He also made an enormous impact on the world with his bestselling book, *A Brief History of Time.* Crippled by Lou Gehrig's disease, he is confined to a wheelchair and uses a computer to speak.

His schedule includes speaking engagements at universities all over the world. His talks are brilliant and filled with humor. I look forward to meeting him when he speaks at UC Santa Barbara, not far from my home in Montecito. I hope to talk to him.

I read a book entitled *The Diving Bell and the Butterfly,* written by a Frenchman, Jean-Dominique Bauby. He was in his early forties, the energetic editor of *Elle* magazine, when following an automobile accident, he suffered a massive stroke. He was completely and permanently para-lyzed. He was a prisoner in an inert body, unable to talk. The only movement he could make was to blink his left eye; the other eye was paralyzed.

With excruciating patience, he devised a blinking code of letters starting with *e*, the most used, and ending with *w*. Laboriously, he worked every day with an amanuensis. The end product was this book, a memoir of his inner feelings. He felt as if his body was constrained in a diving bell, but his thoughts were like a butterfly in constant movement. He called it the "locked-in syndrome." His book is filled with humor, but the pathos always comes through.

Along with millions of other viewers, I watched Barbara Walters interviewing Dudley Moore. How I loved to listen to him play the piano! Years ago, I first saw Dudley on Broadway with his partner Peter Cook. Later, he made a big hit in the movie *10*, followed by another hit, *Arthur*, in which he played the lovable drunk. I had not seen him for a long time. As I watched him on the TV screen, I gasped. He was haggard, standing shakily. He lost his balance and fell back in his chair. He had difficulty talking. Dudley suffers from the neurological disease PSP (progressive supranuclear palsy). This disease includes symptoms such as falling, difficulty in walking, imbalance, and slurred speech. He agreed to be interviewed because he wanted to help others grapple with the same problem. Barbara asked him what it was that he missed most. A sad smile spread across his face and he moved his fingers awkwardly: "Playing the piano."

John Callahan is a redheaded quadriplegic. He zooms around Portland in his battered wheelchair, always with a smile. He has created a syndicated cartoon, *Pelswick Eggert*. His hero is a lively thirteen-year-old quadriplegic in a wheelchair.

Susan Hauser wrote an article about him in *Parade* magazine (Sunday, May 6, 2001). She points out that he was inspired to do a show by the questions kids ask him. "Do you sleep in the wheelchair?" "Is your girlfriend in a wheelchair?" Callahan wanted to show that people in wheelchairs are basically no different from others.

The actor Robin Williams became intrigued with Callahan. He called him "the funniest man on four wheels." They are now discussing a biographical film in which, of course, Robin would play Callahan.

Callahan is another of the "Little Heroes" in life who help others.

I admire people who deal with their challenges and tragedies.

Such people have always inspired me. Back in 1991–1992, I was writing a novel, *The Gift*. The theme was how a famous horseman dealt with the tragedy of losing a leg. In my research, I talked with Al Rappaport of Performance Prosthetics, a maker of artificial limbs, who introduced me to a client, Jim MacLaren, for whom he was in the process of making a new prosthesis. Jim, a six-foot-five, good-looking athlete studying at Yale was on his way to school when his motorcycle crashed into a bus. He lost his right leg, but that didn't stop him. He still worked as an actor and participated in triathlons, swimming 2.4 miles, bicycling 112 miles, and running 26.2 miles. With his prosthesis, he became the world champion of physically challenged individuals. He never wore a cosmetic prosthesis, just a steel rod inserted in his shoe. He saw no need to cover it up. I admired him. We became friends. He often stayed at our house when he was in Beverly Hills.

On his first visit, Fifi was concerned that he would not be able to walk up the narrow steps to the guest bedroom. "Fifi," I said, "if he can win a triathlon with one leg, he will make those steps."

One summer, Jim was participating in a triathlon in Orange County. He asked me to watch him race. It was a Sunday, the last day of the event. I couldn't go, so we arranged to meet at my house the next day.

But the next day, I visited him in the hospital.

He looked up at me. "Kirk, what are the odds of my having two accidents like this in five years?" He was completely paralyzed. He had broken his neck, and to prevent his head from moving, he wore a steel crown called a striker frame. He told me how it happened. As he was speeding through the streets on his bicycle, the final event of the race, a pickup truck got in his way. He flew thirty feet through the air, lost his helmet, and smashed his head against an iron lamppost. He was smiling, but I had to go into the hall to cry.

Jim, again, dealt with his handicap. He did therapeutic exercises every day, and always had a sense of humor. One day, sitting in his electric wheelchair by my pool, he grabbed me and sat me on his lap. "Wanna ride?" He pushed the joystick forward, and we spun around the swimming pool. When he stopped, we were both laughing.

"This accident has been a gift to me," he said. I was shocked.

Kirk Douglas

My friend Jim MacLaren, who gave me a ride in his wheelchair.

"What do you mean?" I asked quizzically.

"I consider it a stroke of luck."

"What are you saying, a stroke of luck?"

"Yes, I was lucky, it changed me. I didn't like the guy I used to be."

I looked at him in astonishment.

*   *   *

My Stroke of Luck

These days Jim spends his time giving inspirational talks to people afflicted with any of an array of physical challenges. Why is it that some people get stronger with adversity, while others shrink?

Eight.

Oral Aerobics

"Your speech therapist is here."

It was my wonderful wife kicking me out of bed.

"Start working."

I was still feeling depressed, but I decided to crawl out of my cave. I wiped away my tears, blew my nose, and went out to meet her. I felt embarrassed, a child learning to talk.

My speech therapist, a tall pleasant lady, Nancy Sadat, smiled at me. I tried to say, "What's a stroke?" I was relieved that she understood me. She made sense of my garbled words.

"We call it a brain attack. Some area of the brain has been injured and is not capable of functioning as it did before. It's caused by a blockage or rupture of a blood vessel to the brain. The damage to the body—whether you can talk or walk—depends on the extent and severity of the damage to the brain. Why does it happen? We don't know. A stroke is a mysterious accident."

"Myster . . ." I couldn't say the word.

"Mysterious?"

I nodded.

"It happens suddenly, without any warning. You were lucky."

"Yeah," I succeeded in interjecting, pleased with even a small word.

"Your wife got you to the hospital in a short time," she began again.

"So?" I tried to converse.

She looked at me and measured her words: "Mr. Douglas, immediate care saved your life."

My brain—or what was left of it—was whirling. There it was again, death. I don't want to die. I cringed, hoping she didn't see my fear; fear that my luck had run out.

Nancy interrupted my thoughts: "Mel Tormé says hello."

"What?"

"He's my client."

"A stroke?"

"Yes."

He was one of my favorite singers. With a voice they described as "the Velvet Fog." I liked him very much, but we hadn't seen each other for a couple of years, and I didn't know he'd had a stroke.

"How's he doing?"

"He can't swallow."

I looked at her quizzically.

"The stroke affected his esophagus, and he's unable to swallow."

"How does he eat?"

"Through a tube inserted into his stomach."

I shuddered; I was almost grateful for my speech impediment. Things could always be worse.

"Say hello to Mel." Every week we talked together through our speech therapist.

I worked hard, grateful that I could swallow. First, there were oral aerobics. Their purpose was to loosen my lips, tongue, and cheeks. Voice exercises included going up and down the scale with different sounds.

I was told to massage my right cheek often, try to utter a list of words, speak slowly to permit the tongue to get around the sounds, articulate, emphasize the ending of words. I could do all those things.

I was sure that in about three months, I would be speaking perfectly. Oh boy, was I wrong.

I practiced every day. I started in the morning with my televised exercise tape of oral aerobics. This required an assortment of grimaces involving lips and tongue, to loosen me up. The beautiful girl on the screen led the exercises. We worked together every day. There are many devices to help exercise the mouth—different-shaped spoons, gadgets with rubber bands. I tried them all:

- Open your mouth wide and yawn. Turn the yawn into a sigh. Repeat ten times.

- Count to ten in your highest pitch and then count to ten in your lowest pitch.

- Pretend you have peanut butter stuck to the roof of your mouth. Tighten your lips and draw your tongue against the roof of your mouth and suck off all the peanut butter.

- Stick out your tongue as far as you can. Hold it for five seconds. Repeat ten times.

I do these exercises while driving to the office. If you try them, be warned: You must be careful to concentrate at the wheel. Also, be prepared when you stop at a red light and you're doing your exercises—especially the one where you stick out your tongue as far as you can for five seconds. Ignore the people in the other cars laughing at you. I don't do much driving—just to the office, the golf course, and of course, to the doctor.

Thankfully, my therapist tried to introduce some humor into our sessions. Try these:

- If you throw a cat out the car window, does she become kitty litter?

- Why do kamikaze pilots wear helmets?

- How did a fool and his money get together in the first place?

- Do blind Eskimos have Seeing Eye sled dogs?

- Sex is like air. It's not important unless you aren't getting any.

My frustration at trying to communicate by speech is always there. Since my stroke I have developed an appreciation for language, an avenue of communication that is the richest and most nuanced (not to mention appropriate) means to express our inner thoughts and feelings. But the more I concentrate on our English language, I wonder how do people, without strokes, ever learn to speak it? The spelling is so crazy!

So many words spelled the same can have different meanings and different sounds. Look at these sentences:

- The bandage was *wound* around the *wound*.

- The farm was used to *produce produce*.

- The dump was so full that it had to *refuse* more *refuse*.

- He could *lead* if he would get the *lead* out.

- When shot at, the *dove dove* into the bushes.

- I did not *object* to the *object*.

- The insurance was *invalid* for the *invalid*.

- They were too *close* to the door to *close* it.

- The buck *does* funny things when the *does* are present.

- To help with planting, the farmer taught his *sow* to *sow*.

- The *wind* was too strong to *wind* the sail.

- After a *number* of injections, my jaw got *number*.

- Upon seeing the *tear* in the painting, I shed a *tear*.

- I had to *subject* the *subject* to a series of tests.

- How can I *intimate* this to my most *intimate* friend?

I think this was done to be mean to stroke victims.

Then, as every third grader knows, there are the words that sound the same when spoken, but are spelled differently when written:

He threw *the ball* through *the window,* too, *and when it broke in* two, *he felt terrible when he saw the damage he had done* to *the brand*-new car . . . *who* knew *he could throw a ball so well?!*

As you regain your speech, the spelling can confuse you.

I always have trouble with my *S*s. One night some friends took me to an Italian restaurant (I love pasta). In ordering my dinner, I couldn't say "spaghetti." All I could say was "paghetti." We all laughed.

That week, I concentrated on *S*. This is how you say it: "Spread your lips, teeth almost touching, tongue flat against your bottom teeth and make the *S* sound. Remember to place your tongue lightly on the front teeth and allow the air to exit over the tip. Do not allow the tongue to rest between your teeth for any of the sibilant sounds.

Practice for ten minutes, twice a day. Say the words with care. Allow time for your lips and tongue to get around."

Did you get all that? Now try it. Of course, with practice, it becomes automatic.

Not long after, I was in the same restaurant and there were my friends at a corner table. I walked over to them, leaned down, and said, "Spaghetti, *s*paghetti, *s*paghetti." And then, haughtily, walked away, my heart filled with the *S* of smiles.

I had more trouble with the word "is" than President Clinton, until I realized that "is" is *iz*. I couldn't say Mexico until I realized it was *Meksiko*. One exercise helped, but drove me crazy: "A sick sparrow sang six sad spring songs sitting sighing under a simmering sun." I don't know if I could have handled that *before* my stroke!

Constantly, I had to remind myself, "Don't lose your sense of humor." When I tried to talk with one of my sons and he said, "What did you say, Dad?," I answered in astonishment, very slowly, "Don't . . . you . . . speak . . . English?" We both laughed.

Michael was very sympathetic. We had been planning to do a movie together.

"Dad, don't worry. We'll do the movie, just keep working with your speech therapist."

"Michael, why don't *you* work with my speech therapist?"

He looked at me.

"And when you talk like I talk, we'll do the movie," I challenged.

We both roared.

Nine.

Don't Forget the Pooper-Scooper

Oral exercises were not enough. I had to do physical exercises as well to increase my strength. The stroke had weakened my right side.

I have always been athletic. In college, at St. Lawrence University in New York, I was the undefeated wrestling champion. That helped me to do my own stunts in movies. I remember watching the stuntman at a distance, wearing my wardrobe doing fancy horse mounts as my character. I didn't like that. I wanted to do it myself. I kept watching and then it came to me. "I can do it," I told the director. "Get me a small one-foot trampoline." The trick in any mount is to get your ass high enough. Grasp the pummel, get an added lift by springing from the trampoline, and voilà! I was on the horse's back. I practiced scissor mounts and rump mounts, all gracefully executed. I don't think I was popular with the stuntman.

I used my newfound equestrian talents in a picture with John Wayne. Everybody called him Duke, but I called him John. He asked me why I never called him Duke. "Maybe Prince or King . . . but Duke? Too low . . . I'll call you John." I think he liked that.

I enjoyed working with John. In *The War Wagon*, Wayne was getting bored by people telling him how adept Douglas was with a horse. He was being interviewed by a reporter who asked, "Is Kirk really that good with a horse?" John scowled: "Bullshit, he can't even get on a horse without a trampoline!" But in spite of that, we were always good friends, and did three movies together.

I enjoyed the challenge of learning to do new things. Juggling for *The Juggler*, fancy rope skipping for *The Champion*, walking the oars in *The Vikings*—not so difficult when you get the rhythm. Fancy gunslinging followed easily from my juggling. My wrestling days in college and carnivals gave me the ability to handle myself in brawls. I took my body for granted. But, things change.

Today, I still exercise—my routine consists of all kinds of stretching, twenty to twenty-five push-ups, twenty to twenty-five curls with a ten-pound weight. If you don't get your blood flowing and your heart pumping, you risk another stroke. I try to strengthen my bad knees by jogging in the pool.

Kirk Douglas

Two tough guys fighting the war in In Harm's Way. *Wayne was tougher.*

And, I play golf. At first, I couldn't even think of ever playing the game again, but after a few months, I was strong enough to play three holes, then nine holes, and finally, eighteen holes! My son Michael says my golf swing is better since my stroke because I don't try to kill the ball. But I don't advise having a stroke to improve your game.

The key with exercise of any kind is a daily routine. But don't follow my schedule, which was designed for my personal needs—get a qualified doctor or trainer to lay out the best exercise routine for you.

One of the best forms of exercise is walking at a brisk pace for twenty to forty minutes. I can't do that because of my knees, but I do love to walk the dogs.

A stroke makes you a more considerate person. About ten o'clock at night, my wife would say, "I'm going to take the dogs out." I'd answer, "No, no, I'll do it." I get off my back and call the dogs. Danny is the older yellow Lab and Foxy is the feisty younger dog, with a beautiful dark red coat. Danny is a Jewish dog, but he doesn't know it, so don't tell him. His real name is Danielovitch, my original Russian name, but we call him Danny for short. Every night before going to bed, I walk with them in the garden singing, *"Who let the dogs out?"*

While they do their thing I search for the most

beautiful rose. There are so many. Have you ever picked a perfect rose in the moonlight for your lover? You see, stroke victims are very romantic.

But if it is true that "the fragrance always stays on the hand that gives the rose," it can't last long, because I have to get the pooper-scooper to clean up after the dogs.

Ten.
What Is This Thing Called Love?

One of the worst things about being the victim of a stroke is that people feel sorry for you. They want to do things for you. And since you also feel very sorry for yourself, you are more than willing to accept their gifts of kindness.

Your wife says, "Would you like something to drink, honey?"

"Yes, that would be nice."

"Don't get up, sweetheart," she says. "Let me get it for you."

And why not? You've been through a lot. You deserve this loving attention.

Beware of such temptation. Don't let yourself give in.

They may not be aware of it, but well-meaning people are encouraging you to become an invalid. They are enablers. Next thing you know, they'll be feeding you and treating you like a simpering idiot. You can't let them.

I found myself fighting a growing dependency on my wife. "No, honey, I'll get it myself. And while I'm up, would you like a drink, too?"

A small thing, but it means a lot. When you do that, you feel stronger. You have accomplished something, no matter how small. That's how you cling to your willpower, and you need every ounce of your willpower to get better.

I realized that I could not give in to the temptation to become a sedentary child tended by others. I had to take control. I had to will myself to get better. I had to fight for it.

People have to learn how to deal with you. My wife had to make a big adjustment. The best thing she did was forbid me to complain. When I would declare morosely, "Anne, I'm not speaking well today," she'd answer, "Oh, no, honey, you're just temporarily out of order."

Anne knows the perfect balance, when to help and when not. She takes control and protects me from difficult daily decisions, makes me comfortable, endures my changing moods, encourages me to become a better person. I have always admired Anne, and have learned so much from her about living an authentic life. But I began to understand love the day Anne found a lump in her breast, years before I had my stroke.

I took her to the hospital immediately. The doctor said it had to be removed. I sat in the waiting room nervously while she was on the operating table. It seemed like an eternity, but finally the doctor entered, still attired in his operating gear. He didn't look happy.

"How did it go?"

The doctor hesitated.

"Tell me!" I insisted.

"Kirk, we removed the lump, but . . . "

"But what?"

"The cancer was spreading toward the lymph gland."

My mouth started to get dry. "What does that mean?"

"Well, if it goes into the lymph gland, she

could die." The outside traffic seemed to drown out the silence of the room.

"How is Anne now?" *Anne, Anne,* echoing from somewhere inside me.

"She's still on the table—under anesthesia."

"Well, do something!"

"We have to ask your permission."

"For what . . . For what?"

"Try to calm down, Kirk."

"My wife is dying, and you want me to be calm?"

"She isn't dying."

"What can you do?"

"I can remove all the cancer by cutting off her breast." There. It was out.

I had a sudden impulse to strangle him.

He's a doctor, and all that he can do is mutilate my wife? I turned away, tried not to cry, and thought of her beautiful breasts. The ground was slipping out from under me.

"Kirk, I know it's difficult for you. I can sew her up and you can discuss it with her. That won't be easy for Anne. Right now she's still under anesthesia."

"Doc." I turned and looked directly into his eyes. "If it was your wife, what would you do?"

He looked straight at me and said without hesitation, "I would remove her breast. Now."

I sagged into a chair and said, almost inaudibly, "All right, do it." But he heard me. He patted me on the shoulder and then I heard the door open and close.

Countless times I asked myself if I had made the right decision. Was there one? Anne reassured me that I had. But for a long time, she made sure that I didn't see that part of her. Did she fear that I wouldn't find her attractive?

For a long, long time, we made love every night. We had overcome an obstacle, survived cancer, survived life. There were times I felt like my tongue had been cut off. Anne helped me find the words, and our love became stronger.

Anne immersed herself in helping women with breast cancer. In a speech before the Breast Resource Center she said, "Years ago, breast cancer was not something you told people you had. After my surgery, I looked at myself in the mirror. I saw myself as a deformed person. It took me a long time and a lot of sessions with my support group to realize, hey, I am alive! Now it's wonderful to be able to talk about it and cry openly. It is very comforting to share my feelings, even with strangers."

People marry because they fall head over heels in love. Often, when people marry, they have mistaken infatuation, obsession, deep friendship, or good sex for love. But those things are not love. Love must have a chance to grow and blossom. Love must pass the test of overcoming

Kirk Douglas

My partner, my friend, my lover—Anne.

obstacles. Love, like a work of art or a fine wine, must also pass the test of time.

Rilke, the poet, once said: "Love consists in this, that two solitudes protect and touch and greet each other." Two people in love should never become one. There must be a space in togetherness. True love, real love, is born of respect for another person. It is given and received with a fullness of self that can only be drawn from an individual and separate soul. And the loneliness in solitude is compensated for by a rich and abiding togetherness in love.

It took me a long time to learn that differences between Anne and me enhance our love. We must respect each other and allow each other to be what each of us, separately, is. Never try to change your spouse.

Having people in your life that you love leaves you vulnerable. There are prices exacted for having a heart open to love. And yet a good love, a love that is worth sharing, keeping, and fighting for, is a love that is worth risking a broken heart for. In my life, I have been lucky to find that love. Even though I almost lost her.

Forty-eight years ago I was shooting *20,000 Leagues Under the Sea*. Saturday night, after shooting, Anne and I flew to Las Vegas to get married. The ceremony took place in a suite in Caesars Palace, led by a man in a western hat called Honest John Lytell. He spoke with a southern accent. When he said to Anne, "Repeat after me, I take Kirk as my lawful wedded husband," my nervous Parisian wife said, "I take Kirk as my *awful* wedded husband." That almost broke up the wedding. Anne was thinking of "full of awe." We concluded with the phone ringing to tell us that Sinatra was holding up the show until we arrived. He was saying, "Hurry up!"

Anne and I should have had a better wedding. I will propose to her again, and if she says yes, we will have a big second wedding in two more years. This time celebrating our fiftieth anniversary. I plan to make it even a bigger event than Michael and Catherine's nuptials. I'd better start practicing the wedding vows now: *I* do . . . I *do* . . . *I do!*

Eleven.

I Face My Public

Before my stroke, the Academy of Motion Picture Arts and Sciences had voted to award me an Oscar for Lifetime Achievement. I was very pleased and grateful. This particular award is not given often. But would I be ready?

I kept working with my speech therapist three times a week. One session, I asked her, "I haven't heard from Mel, how is he?" She paused and looked at me.

"What happened?" I asked.

"Mel Tormé died two days ago."

That stunned me. Wow! You can die from a stroke! But Mel couldn't swallow. I was lucky. I thought of Mel singing the song that he wrote, "The Christmas Song." I could hear his mellow voice: "Chestnuts roasting on an open fire, Jack Frost nipping at your nose . . . " It made me very sad.

But time goes on. Oscar night was drawing nearer. Every day I did both my oral aerobics and physical exercises religiously. I even tried to read the Torah out loud to my rabbi. I was clutching at straws. Anything to help.

Three months passed and I still didn't see any improvement. How can I talk in front of all those people? My speech therapist thought I was making progress, but I didn't believe her. As the night of the Oscars drew near, I became frantic.

"Michael, you accept for me."

"No way," my son answered emphatically. "You will go up on that stage if you have to crawl." And he walked away.

There was no way out. I had to do it. I would accept it and say two words, "Thank you." In front of the mirror I practiced: "*thank* you, thank *you*, *thank you*." To get the *th* sound, you have to put your tongue . . . ah, forget it.

Oscar night, a limousine drove a quivering Kirk directly to the stage door. My family had left earlier to get seats in the audience. Alone, I was ushered to producer Quincy Jones's office. Oprah was there, looking ravishing in her fine gown. I tried to make a joke. "If I were twenty years younger, you wouldn't have a chance." She smiled. I don't think she knew what the hell I said.

Then they led me, stumbling, through the backstage darkness to a chair in the wings. Nervously, I sat there. I heard a voice, my voice. I looked at the backstage monitor. It was a scene from *Spartacus*. I was speaking so clearly.

"That night you walked into my cell, and I looked at you . . . touched your skin and felt your hair."

I felt a kiss on my cheek—Sharon Stone. Another kiss—Whoopi Goldberg. Mel Gibson tiptoed over. He didn't kiss me but wished me luck.

I heard the voice of Steven Spielberg onstage. *"We're celebrating and honoring Kirk Douglas tonight because he's done nearly everything on film. He's directed, he's produced, and in the process he's helped to hammer the blacklist to pieces."*

That made me tingle. Breaking the blacklist—the one thing that I was really proud of.

"Most stars of his stature are shaped out of mythic clay. Kirk Douglas never chose that. He doesn't have a single role that makes him unique; instead, he has a singular honesty—a drive to be

inimitable. That's what animates all his roles from Spartacus to Vincent Van Gogh."

Wow! Now I was listening intently. I was enjoying it. I closed my eyes and let his words caress me.

"His characters weren't bigger than life, they were life reconverted—something we all could identify with, something that would touch us out there in the dark, something that gave the dark a life and a light of its own."

I was lapping it up.

"Ladies and gentlemen, Kirk Douglas."

I almost fell off my chair. Someone helped me, and whispered, "A billion people will be watching you on TV!" That didn't help.

I stood up, braced my shoulders, took a deep breath, and tried to walk on like Spartacus. I hugged Spielberg and then turned to the audience. I blinked my eyes—two thousand people! On their feet cheering! All this to hear me say "thank you"? Spielberg

Kirk Douglas

The first time I spoke in public after my stroke—receiving an Oscar.

gave me the Oscar. It was heavy! They were still standing. Waves of applause engulfed me. I can't just say thank you, I thought. I looked over the audience. Carrying my Oscar, I took tentative steps to the microphone. I dared to look out at the finally settled audience. To the right, I could make out my four sons—Eric, Peter, Joel, and Michael—and my wife, Anne, all in a row, staring at me. I thought of the lessons I learned with my speech therapist. Pause . . . breathe . . . swallow . . . articulate.

I started slowly: "I see my four sons." I pointed. "They're proud of the old man." The audience responded with a big laugh. They understood me! I spotted my wife covering her face and sobbing—as she later said, ruining a twenty-five-dollar makeup job. I held up the Oscar. "Anne, this belongs to you. I love you."

The audience roared their appreciation. I was soaking it up. I didn't want to leave. I hadn't said thank you yet. I paused, took a deep breath and swallowed. "Thank you for fifty wonderful years in the wonderful world of moviemaking."

I bowed, thunderous applause engulfing me. With my arm around Spielberg, I walked off. Again, a standing ovation. I was dumbfounded by the reaction. I couldn't believe it.

They understood me. They really understood me.

Confucius said long ago, "A journey of a thousand miles must start with a single step." I accomplished the first important step in my rehabilitation: I spoke before the public, my public. In spite of an impediment, they could make out what I was saying.

This fortified another rule for overcoming any disability: Never give up . . . keep trying! That goes in my "Manual." Letters, faxes, and phone calls came pouring in. One letter startled me. It was from King Hussein, the ruler of Jordan. He was one of the billions watching the Oscar show. He invited me to visit him in Jordan and see the country.

My four boys and me carrying Anne and the Oscar.

Of course, I couldn't make such a long trip, but I thanked him for his kindness. I needed it. His letter encouraged me to work harder with my speech therapist, exercise more, and talk with other people besides my family.

When I first heard that King Hussein had died, I felt I had lost a friend. He would never know how much his letter helped me.

Twelve.

My Pacemaker

Again, I was in the hospital. This time to replace my pacemaker.

Yes, I have carried a pacemaker in my chest for over ten years. Have you ever seen one? It is smaller than a silver dollar but thicker. Inside is a battery connected to a lead that goes through the veins to the ventricle of my heart. If my heartbeat is less than fifty, it kicks in and stimulates the heartbeat.

After ten years, the battery was running low. How did I know?

Every month, the pacemaker is monitored by an office in New York. I am in Beverly Hills, three thousand miles away, when the phone rings and someone says, "Are you ready, Mr. Douglas?"

"Just a minute."

I open a small box by my bed which contains a battery, a cradle for the phone, and wires attached to two bracelets. I put the bracelets on— one on each arm—flip the button to start the power in the box.

"I'm ready."

"Put the phone on the cradle and count to thirty." I do it.

I pick up the phone and she says, "That was fine. Now put the phone back in the cradle and place the magnet on your pacemaker and count to twenty."

I do it.

"That was fine. Have a good day, Mr. Douglas."

The whole procedure doesn't take more than four minutes. A report comes to my doctor listing how often my heart uses the pacemaker implanted in my chest. It also measures the strength of the battery, which, after ten years, was getting low. It had to be changed. Imagine that.

Reluctantly, Dr. Gold agreed to the replacement of the pacemaker. Even a minor operation requires stopping the intake of Coumadin, a medication to thin the blood, for a short period.

I take certain medications daily to avoid another stroke: I take doses of Hytrin to help keep the blood pressure down; Coumadin, the most important medication, helps to prevent blood clotting. A clot travels up an artery leading to the brain. It blocks the flow of blood to that section of the brain. This can cause a minor stroke or a massive stroke.

A stroke makes you bruise easily. I grow tired of finding a bruise on my body every time I knock it against something. You must try to avoid getting a cut because you bleed profusely.

My knees are in bad shape from the helicopter crash. I am a candidate for new knees, but such an operation would necessitate cutting off the Coumadin for several days. This is dangerous. My doctor advised me to suffer the pain in my knees and not have the operation.

But my pacemaker couldn't wait. The battery was dangerously low and had to be changed. Reluctantly, my doctor agreed to take me off of the Coumadin a few days before the operation. I remember lying on the table as they applied the anesthetic. Then they cut me open and exchanged the little instrument in my chest connected to a wire inserted into my heart. I felt so helpless lying there. The prospect of dying haunted me. I drifted off hearing the words of my mother. . . . *Don't be afraid, it happens to everyone.*

Thirteen.
Lights, Camera, Action!

A knock on my door and Fifi entered holding a large envelope. "This was delivered by hand." I turned off the television and opened it. Inside I found a script! A movie script: *Diamonds*. I was astounded. They wanted me to play the lead!

My first thought was: I can't act in a movie

again! But it didn't take me long to change my mind: Why not? Let's give the character a stroke. Who can play a stroke victim better than me? I accepted. I studied the script for days. But when the starting date grew closer, I was filled with stage fright. "Anne, I don't think I'll be able to talk."

My wife looked at me with disdain. "When the camera begins to roll, you will begin to talk."

And I did.

But first, I called my friend Lauren Bacall. I wanted her to be in the picture. "Betty"—friends call her Betty—"I have a great role for you in a movie that I'm going to do."

"You're going to make a movie?" she asked in surprise.

"Yeah, I'm going to make a movie! I am an actor, remember?"

"Oh yeah, I remember." Bacall sarcasm. "What's the role?"

"You can play the pants off it," I taunted.

"But what's the role?" she insisted.

"The madam of a whorehouse."

After some expletives, she agreed to do it and played it superbly.

We shot the picture in Reno, Nevada. All through the filming, I forgot about depression, and depression forgot about me. I was deeply involved with my character, Harry. I incorporated much of my own life into the role. Harry was a boxer: the stroke was caused by an accident in the ring. This enabled the director to use shots from *The Champion*, in which I played a twenty-seven-year-old boxer.

Diamonds came out, starring Kirk Douglas! I was an actor again! The audience understood me. They liked the picture. Stroke victims, their families, and stroke organizations were especially fascinated by *Diamonds*.

You see, a stroke is a disease that people

often hide. They feel guilty, embarrassed, humiliated. When they talk, they feel that people look at them as if they are stupid. *Diamonds* helped to bring this illness out in the open; people began to talk more about strokes. I answered the many letters and calls I received from victims and their families.

". . . I had a stroke, which affected my left side and writing ability. My goal is to recover as well as I have seen you recently on TV."

". . . Don't be discouraged, you can only get better."

". . . It is a tremendous inspiration to me to know that you have been affected by a stroke and have recovered to the extent that you have made another movie."

". . . You gave me hope that someday I'll be back on my feet again."

". . . Three years ago I had a stroke. Then I had a heart attack. Then I had a severed heel. There ain't no justice. But this year, I have a goal to walk again and to drive again."

". . . Having heard of your stroke and how you have advanced in life is very inspiring to me, giving me a reason to live."

And there were many, many other letters. I answered them and tried to help the people who wrote them lessen their fears.

I was getting many requests to give talks. How did I handle my affliction? How did I keep a sense of humor? How did I handle depression? Reluctantly, I pushed myself out of my cocoon and flew to San Francisco to speak to a convention of speech therapists. They helped me greatly, and I wanted to do something to say thank you.

This is what I said:

When you have a stroke you must talk slowly—to be understood. And I've discovered that when I talk slowly [big pause] people listen! [Laughter.] They think I'm going to say something important. [Laughter.] Do you understand me when I speak? That's amazing. Because right after my stroke, all I could do was babble like a baby. But I worked hard with my speech therapist, and in a few months I could talk as well as my three-year-old grand-daughter, Kelsey.

But I kept working, and one day I said, "Kelsey, say 'transcontinental.' " She couldn't say it. And I left her in the dust. [Laughter.] Now I talk like a six-year-old. Grandchildren are wonderful. You play with them a few hours and then you run home. You know I have four sons and I've worked with all of them except Michael. Now we are developing a script to do together. I'm really excited to be making a movie with my famous son. If I knew he was going to be that famous, I would have been nicer to him when he was young.

I gained confidence. I began making more speeches. I became cocky. Here's how I repaid my wife, who has been such a great help to me. In a speech, here's what I said about her:

My wife has been a great help to me. But she believes in tough love. Last week I said, "Honey, I would like to have breakfast in bed tomorrow." Her answer: "Breakfast in bed? Then sleep in the kitchen!" She tries to help me, but sometimes she becomes exasperated. One day, after an argument, she said, "I'm going to leave you!" I looked at her, "If you ever leave me, I'm going with you!" But she's a big help. Before I came on to talk to you, I said, "Honey, I'm nervous. Will they understand my speech?" She said, "Do you have anything important to say?" Well, I may not have anything important to say, but I've received many requests to give a talk. People like to hear slurred speech. I'm going to try to make strokes fashionable. [I'll say anything for a laugh!]

Fred DeCordova had a stroke. He used to be the director of Johnny Carson's *Tonight Show*. I knew him for years. His wife called me. He was depressed. I visited him and tried to cheer him up.

"How old are you, Fred?"

"Ninety-one."

"Ninety-one?"

"Yeah."

"Don't you ever read the obituary columns?"

"No, never."

"Well, you should, you're way ahead of the game!"

I got him laughing before I left.

Many people contact me to talk to their family members who have difficulty dealing with a stroke. It's much easier for a person with a stroke to help another suffering the same malady.

A friend of mine for fifty years would come and visit me in the hospital after my helicopter crash. He came to see me again at the hospital when I had my stroke. Recently, he, too, was rushed to the hospital with a stroke. For several weeks, he was in intensive care and I couldn't visit him. He couldn't swallow and had to be fed by a tube attached to his stomach. Of course his speech was greatly impaired. When he was moved to a private room, I went to see him. He looked pitiful. I thought of the people who came to visit me when I was in that state. Most of them didn't know what to say, and spoke as if my brain was impaired. I could quickly see that my friend's brain was functioning normally. He tried to speak to me with his slurred speech. I said, "Listen, after you work with a speech therapist, you will be talking the way you always talk—too much!" This brought a faint smile. "And I will go with you to take lessons from the therapist, but don't be mad at me if I get to be at the head of the class." For the first time, I could almost see the beginnings of a laugh. It made me sad, but I remembered that humor is one of the best medicines you can give anyone who is suffering.

His family wanted to keep his illness a secret. Why? Somehow a stroke is looked upon as the "plague." If you have cancer you are treated with more dignity. I went home that night feeling very sad for my friend. How could I help him?

My Stroke of Luck

My friend was a great conversationalist with a wonderful sense of humor. He was always telling a joke or twisting everything into a gag. I had to find a way to help him.

It's not always easy to help a person who's had a stroke. When a very famous director, John Schlesinger, had a stroke, one of his friends, Diana, my ex-wife, called me and asked for my help. "Talk to him," she said. "You can make him feel better."

I called him at the hospital. His assistant told me that he didn't want to talk to me. I understood that feeling. At the beginning of my stroke, I didn't want to talk to anybody either. So I left a message that if he ever wanted to talk to me, please call.

Not long ago, my friend Jack Valenti called to tell me that his friend Lloyd Bentsen had had a stroke. Maybe I could help him. I wrote him a letter, and his wife sent me a very warm reply. Then I wrote again, saying that I wanted to talk to him. I got no answer, but I understand.

Another letter from my ex-wife, Diana:

"... *I hesitate to ask another favor after you so kindly tried to contact John Schlesinger to no avail. But I have just learned that Julie Harris had a stroke and lost the power of speech.*

She is in the hospital in Boston and refuses to see anyone. She is deeply, deeply depressed. It must be the most terrifying thing for an actor to lose their voice.

I'm sure it will be a big help to her if you dropped her a line to give her some hope. . . ."

So I wrote Julie Harris a letter:

Dear Julie,

Three years ago I had a stroke. I didn't want to

see anybody. I didn't want anyone to see me. I just lay in bed in a dark depression.

I think depression is the most difficult thing to deal with. You must deal with it and realize that things could always be worse.

I am writing a book that I hope will help stroke survivors. Maybe it will help others to deal with depression. May I send you a copy?

The memory of all that you have done with your career fills me with gratitude.

Don't give up!

Love,

Kirk

Fourteen.
I Hate Technology!

It's very difficult for me to talk on the phone. I'm embarrassed when people don't understand me. I never carry a cell phone. But when I walk down the street, what is everybody doing? They all stroll along with a box jammed up against their ear. They are talking to someone far away. Cars whiz by and the drivers are arguing or joking with a ghost. I don't like it. I began to hate technology.

My wife bought me a beautiful car. She was very happy as the salesman drove up to show me the unique features. I sat next to him and he pushed a button.

"What number, please," said the car. I opened the door and walked out. "I don't want the car." My wife and the salesman were aghast. "Why?"

"I don't want a car that talks to me." After many remonstrations and explanations, I held firm. "I don't want the car!"

Now Anne drives the talking car and I drive her old coupe. We are both happy. I kid you not: Technology bothers me.

Sometimes, I sit in front of my TV and keep pushing a button very rapidly. A hundred different stations are at my instantaneous control, completely audible. They come from all over the world. Now it is possible to have a thousand channels. When will they stop?

All my life I've had a hard time comprehending how a voice on the telephone can be carried through wires. But now, "Look, Ma, no wires." Sometimes, I sit in my room, look around, and breathe the air. And I wonder, are television pictures beaming into my lungs? I have heard of people who can tune in a radio with the metal fillings in their teeth. I'm afraid to breathe!

Maybe people are going to say that my stroke affected my brain, or maybe I'm just plain dumb. But how many people truly understand the technology they use every day?

Maybe I am just jealous that all these cars, computer and cell phone users, and even my very own pacemaker are all communicating so effortlessly while I struggle with every word.

Fifteen.

I Believe in Miracles

Even those who can honestly say they understand technology cannot claim to understand the human body. Considering we have been dissecting, manipulating, and inhabiting it for centuries, we comprehend so little of its workings!

We know what causes a stroke—a cerebral hemorrhage that is a blood spill in the brain OR a lack of blood supply to the brain. Which one happened to me? Did a blood vessel burst in my brain? Or did a clot block blood flow?

People in general know so little about a stroke. What did I know before it happened to me? Nothing. The seemingly simple process of instantaneously expressing in speech a thought, image, or idea that originates in the brain is so utterly complicated, yet it is only one small miracle in the human body. Yes, it is a miracle. And miracles come only from God.

The great scientist Albert Einstein said, "There are two ways to see the world. One is to see nothing as a miracle, the other is to see everything as a miracle." Einstein believed in God. And if you believe in miracles, you believe in God.

Since my stroke, I have begun to see so many miracles all around me. I look out of the window in my room: verdant grass, silver-tipped oak leaves, tall palm trees gently swaying as they reach to the sky, masses and masses of roses. All colors, so many shapes, exquisite fragrances. I became aware of the many, many miracles in life that we take for granted: the changes of season, the formation of clouds in the sky, the sunset, the sunrise. Where does the breeze come from, a strong wind, the rain, a sudden rainbow, that ever-changing moon, the snow? The trees move gently, laden with so many golden oranges, waiting to be picked.

I remember a favorite prayer I read in a Hebrew prayer book, translated into English:

Oh God, how can we know you? Where can we find you? You are as close to us as breathing, yet you are farther than the farthermost star. You are as mysterious as the vast solitude of night, yet as familiar to us as the light of the sun.

This expresses how I feel about God. I recite this prayer every day.

I feel like a child again seeing the world for the first time. I am still alive. Isn't that a miracle? I am an eighty-three-year-old stroke survivor, an actor who is still working, a father, a grandfather, a husband, a man . . . I feel like dancing!

So young again! Thank God! Yes, thank God, but how? I got it. In Judaism, a boy is confirmed when he is thirteen years old. It represents his entrance into manhood. The ceremony is called a bar mitzvah. Saturday morning, you are called up to read from the Torah in the synagogue. You make a speech, and then there is a festive lunch with all your friends and family.

In the Torah, it is written that a man's life span is seventy years. After that, he begins all over again. I am eighty-three years old—thirteen years after seventy. So, I am thirteen again. I will thank God by having my second bar mitzvah.

At first, my friends thought I was joking. But again, I studied the required Hebrew prayers, and I was ready.

Sinai Temple was overflowing with friends, curious to see my second bar mitzvah. I was surrounded by my sons, my grandchildren, my wife, and my ex-wife. Michael brought a beautiful girl, Catherine Zeta-Jones, who later became his wife. So many of my colleagues were there. Karl Malden, Larry King, Red Buttons, Don Rickles, Roddy McDowall, and even the mayor of Los Angeles, Richard Riordan.

After the service, I made a speech:

You know, this old tallis—the prayer shawl that I'm wearing—I wore on my first bar mitzvah seventy years ago. And if my mother is looking down and watching us, she will recognize it.

Kirk Douglas

With my wonderful daughter-in-law, Catherine Zeta-Jones.

Today I am a man! But it takes time to really become a man and assume your responsibilities in this troubled world.

My Stroke of Luck

I thank all of you for coming here, but I give special thanks to the rabbis that I have learned with. Listen, I know more rabbis than Jews.

Seventy years ago, at thirteen, I had my first bar mitzvah. Boy, was I glad when it was over! No more rulers on the back of my hand when I didn't know all those prayers and rituals. I got through my bar mitzvah and far away from Judaism. I knew I was a Jew, but I kept that to myself.

For years, I became wrapped up in making movie after movie—killing so many Vikings, Romans—knocking people out in the ring— shooting it out with Burt Lancaster.

For years, I was so busy, I had no time to think about anyone but me, me, me.

I had no interest in going to a synagogue, but as a Jew, I did one thing—I always fasted on Yom Kippur. I still worked in movies, but I fasted. And let me tell you, it's not easy making love to Lana Turner on an empty stomach.

Kirk Douglas

Reading the Torah at my second bar mitzvah.

C. S. Lewis wrote, "Pain is God's megaphone to wake up a deaf world." I really didn't know what that meant until I was in a helicopter fifty feet above the ground and we crashed into a small plane. When I woke up in the hospital, I was surprised to find that I was alive, but I was filled with pain and guilt. I learned that two young people in the other plane were killed.

My Stroke of Luck

I was in my seventies. Why was I alive? I was in pain for years and then—I don't know why—I started to study the Torah. I went through the Torah—with a rabbi—twice. I became proud to be a Jew. Maybe too proud because I decided to follow in Moses' footsteps and climb Mount Sinai. Why not? He was my age when he did it.

My wife's reaction: "Climbing a mountain! With your back!"

But she insisted that I have a medical checkup, so Dr. Gold put me on the treadmill, wires attached to my body, and my wife, Anne, watching closely.

After a few minutes, the doctor stopped the treadmill. "Kirk, why don't you stay here. Let your wife climb the mountain." Wives always spoil things.

But the rituals of Judaism don't interest me as much as the spiritual side. Believe what every *religion teaches you—you shall love your neighbor as you love yourself.*

Kirk Douglas

My second bar mitzvah when I was eighty-three years old.

One thing amazed me. There is only one God for all people. Almost every faith believes in the God of Abraham. The Muslims go to Him led by Muhammad. The Christians try to reach the same God following Jesus, and we Jews try to climb the mountain and find God led by Moses. We are all children of God.

Cardinal O'Connor, archbishop of New York, said, "As we begin another millennium in our Jewish-Christian relationship, we will refresh our encounter with a new respect and even love for one another as children of God, working in our own ways, but also working together, that we both remain committed for our fulfillment of God's ways."

Today I am eighty-three—seventy years after my first bar mitzvah allows me to have a second. I can't have a third until I'm 153 years old. Let's not wait that long. Today I am thirteen years old again. I promise, I promise to be a good boy.

I was happy to get a letter from Cardinal O'Connor before he died. He was pleased to learn that I had quoted him.

About a year later, I did my second movie since my stroke. It was an episode on television's *Touched by an Angel*, written by Rabbi Joseph Telushkin. The story was about a man and his grandson, getting bar mitzvahed together. I was ready for that role.

Sixteen.

Sucking Up to God

"Kirk, are you sucking up to God?"

I was startled by the question my friend, Dr. Rick Gold, hurled at me.

"What do you mean?"

"You're eighty-three years old?" he pointed out, unnecessarily.

"So what?"

"You had a helicopter crash?" he taunted.

"Yeah."

"A stroke?"

"Yes."

Undaunted, he pursued, "A pacemaker?"

"What are you getting at?"

"You ever think of dying?" He had me in his sights.

I paused, working hard to outmaneuver whatever was coming. "Albert Schweitzer said that everybody should live their life as if death was sitting on their shoulder."

"I'm not talking to Mr. Schweitzer, I'm talking to you."

"I'm listening!"

"You and Anne do lots of good things—playgrounds for children, centers for old-timers with Alzheimer's, programs to rehabilitate homeless women . . . nice guy."

"So what?" Now I was impatient.

"So that's 'sucking up to God.'" A subtle, slim dart, speeding toward its destination.

I ducked. "Rick, I don't understand you."

"Why did you have a second bar mitzvah? Such a good little boy." He laughed sarcastically.

I was so angry, I couldn't speak. When you have a stroke, any irritation makes speech very difficult.

He answered for me: "So in the next life, He'll be good to you." Mark achieved. Contact. I was stunned. I didn't know how to react. He walked away.

Sucking up to God! I couldn't get that out of my mind. Since my stroke, I had thought a lot about dying. It's hard to accept that death is the end of everything.

I am reminded of that every time I go into the office. Although my home has a few movie mementos, the office walls are covered with

Kirk Douglas

My friend Tony Quinn and I in Last Train from Gun Hill.

posters of the movies I made. I look at them. *Lonely Are the Brave:* Walter Matthau, once so full of life, dead. *Gunfight at the O.K. Corral:* Burt Lancaster, my dear friend, dead. *20,000 Leagues Under the Sea:* James Mason, Paul Lucas, Peter Lorre, dead, dead, dead. *The Bad and the Beautiful:* Lana Turner, so exquisitely beautiful, dead. Her friend Ava Gardner, *Seven Days in May,* dead.

Spartacus: Laurence Olivier, Charles Laughton, Stanley Kubrick . . . that's enough! I don't want to look anymore. But as I turn to go, I find myself looking at a big poster of me staring at my dear friend Tony Quinn. Thank God he was alive. What a good friend, and so funny! I remember him telling me the story of when he married his second wife, Iolanda. They already had two young children together. The morning of the nuptials, the wedding ring was misplaced. Frantically, Tony looked for it while the children watched. Exasperated, he called out to them, "Help me find the ring. Don't you want me to marry your mother?"

A week after I looked at that poster, he died.

Oh how I will miss him. I will always think of Tony dancing in *Zorba*—so strong, so happy, so full of life. I will never lose that image.

A week later, Carroll O'Connor had a heart attack and died. I was stunned. A month earlier,

Kirk Douglas

With Walter Matthau in Indian Fighter. *What a great actor! But he hated horses.*

he had given me a glowing introduction before I spoke at the fund-raising dinner for the John Wayne Cancer Institute.

I liked Carroll. I gave him his first role in a movie, *Lonely Are the Brave.* He played the driver of a truckload of toilets speeding down a rainy highway. I was riding my horse, Whiskey, trying to cross the highway. His truck smashed into both of us. Poor Archie Bunker. He spent so much time fighting drug dealers who caused his son to commit suicide.

I had hardly gotten over his death when Jack Lemmon died—cancer. I couldn't believe it! I was looking forward to our next Sunday poker game with him and his wife, Felicia, at Barbara Sinatra's house. It was strange, his death occurred almost a year to the day that his best friend, Walter Matthau, died. What a blow.

I also gave Walter his first job in a movie: riding a horse, which he hated, in the first production of my company, *The Indian Fighter*. Later, we worked together in *Lonely Are the Brave*. One evening, after work, Walter and I ran into a jewelry salesman wheeling a cart of his wares. "Let's get something for the little women," Walter suggested. (He was very much in love with his wife, Carol.) I agreed. The salesman laid out his wares on the table of my dressing room. I selected an inexpensive pair of earrings for Anne, and Walter picked out a ring for $100. As the salesman was wrapping up our purchases, Walter asked, "How about double or nothing?" As long as I knew Walter, he was a habitual gambler. He would gamble on anything. The vendor agreed, and they tossed a coin. Walter won, but he seemed unhappy. "Let's toss again," he said. I couldn't believe it. Maybe gamblers have an innate wish to lose.

How Walter's death must have affected Jack. They were such good friends—the odd couple. I never worked with Jack. His office was just across the hall from mine, though. I smiled whenever he drove into the parking lot. Some men wear their heart on their sleeve. Jack wore it on his license plate. It read JL ❤ FL. Yes, he was very much in love with Felicia.

Michael and his beautiful Catherine went with me to Jack's memorial, held at Westwood Village

Memorial Park. Michael worked with him in the movie *China Syndrome.*

As we walked to the chapel, we passed the cemetery—no headstones, just plaques lying flat on the green grass. Years ago, Anne and I had bought a double plot here. It made me feel strange. I began to babble. "Marilyn Monroe is buried here. So is Walter Matthau. And today, Jack will join them." There was an awkward pause. No one said anything as we entered the chapel. I still had that strange feeling. I had written often about death, but I didn't believe it. I kept looking at the casket, covered with a huge mound of red roses. This is real. You really die! No more Archie Bunker, no more *Zorba the Greek,* no more *Odd Couple.* Gone, gone, gone.

That night I had a dream. Someone—I don't know who—was looking at a large poster of me with my teeth clenched. A voice said, "Oh, that's Kirk Douglas—he's dead."

But what happens after? (Not the recycling plant!) Would I see my mother? Oh, how I would like to thank her for all of the things that I never thanked her for. I'm so glad she lived to see me become a star after *Champion*. I flew to see her in Albany, New York. I remember the scene vividly: several of her immigrant friends around the table, and my mother beaming at me and saying to the group, "This is my son. The earth trembles when they mention his name."

The Jews have a way with hyperbole, but I liked it. I have been so lucky in life. I come from poverty. My mother didn't read or write. But she taught me a lot. There was a tin box, a *pushke,* on the wall of our kitchen in Amsterdam, New York. We put in pennies from time to time, occasionally a nickel to help other poor people. We lived by the railroad tracks, and if a hobo came to the door, my mother always gave him something. And we didn't have much to eat. I was taught that those who have more should help those who have less. Even a beggar must give something to another beggar who is less well-off.

"Sucking up to God?" Maybe. No doubt I have been too self-centered. Long ago, a friend sadly told me, "Kirk, you're like an ocean liner cutting through the waves, speeding directly to your destination in life. Your friends are like barnacles, clinging to the keel. When the going gets too tough, they drop off." Looking back, I cannot believe that I was once so selfish.

Today I received a fax that reminded me of my faults.

Dear Mr. Douglas,

My father, Paul Wilson, was a friend of yours back in the '40s. I understand that you even lived with the Wilson family when jobs were scarce. My father recently died and amongst his papers we have found old playbills and clippings men-

tioning you. I would be happy to forward copies
if you would like them. Please contact me.

Gale Patron

This shocked me and made me realize the truth: that, indeed, I often did treat friends like barnacles.

I wrote to the daughter of my friend:

Dear Mrs. Patron,
Your fax made me very sad. I loved your father.
He was such a good friend when I first came to
New York to attend dramatic school. I was
waiting for a job with a room in Greenwich Vil-
lage; in the meantime, I had nothing. No place
to live. Paul took me into his house and I
stayed there for I think it was about two weeks.
I'm sure his mother thought I was going to
become "the man who came to dinner." We lost

track of each other when I went to Hollywood, but that's my fault. I know Paul. He wouldn't want to seem to be interfering with my activities. It was really up to me. So many times I would say to myself, "Gee, I must find Paul." At one time I thought someone told me that he had moved to New Jersey, but I was too selfish to follow up on it, because I was concentrating solely on my work and family. When I received your fax, it was like a kick in the ass. Why was I so self-centered? Why did I forget someone who gave me help and friendship when I really needed it? Gale, your father was a great guy, and a gentleman. We had a lot of fun together. Please forgive me for being so self-absorbed that I didn't look up my old friend. I would appreciate any mementos that you care to send.

All my best,

Kirk Douglas

I felt ashamed. Was it sixty years ago? How time flies when you're thinking only of yourself. I would have liked to see Paul again, to thank him for being such a good friend. But now it's too late. I close my eyes and I see a ship speeding through the sea, with barnacles falling off the keel.

My stroke has taught me to be more compassionate, to work harder at my relationships with my loved ones, to value friendship more, to be aware of the world around me, to slow down and to have a richer spiritual life.

Because it was difficult and tiring for me to talk, I began to read much more. I no longer had to spend my time evaluating movie scripts, because few were offered. So I began to read anything and everything about Judaism. The more I studied the Bible, the more intrigued I became with the Jewish people, so stubborn, trying the patience of God. Of course, it was a hard journey through the desert, but they didn't stop complaining: "We

would have been better to stay as slaves in Egypt."
After ten plagues, the parting of the Red Sea, how
could they say that? Moses left for a short time to
climb Mount Sinai and receive the Ten Command-
ments. But oh, no, they couldn't wait. They melted
all of their gold jewelry and made a golden calf to
worship. How could God continue to be patient
with them? With me?

Then came Yom Kippur, the Day of Atone-
ment, the holiday that frightens me. And this was
the first time since my stroke. At the close of this
solemn day, a day of affliction, the Book of Life is
sealed. In it is inscribed who shall live and who
shall die. And I wonder, what category am I in?

Although most of the service was conducted in
Hebrew, the prayer book included the English
translation of the prayers. When I was a kid, the
synagogue prayers were all just in Hebrew. At
Hebrew school, I learned how to read Hebrew, but
I never understood what I was saying.

Now, as I stood up, reading the English translation of the service, I was astonished. Almost every line was an adoration of God:

Praise the Lord to whom all praise is due. Blessed is the Lord our God. Who is like You, Eternal One? Who is like You, Majestic in Holiness? You are the First and the Last. Let the glory of God be extolled, let His great name be hallowed. Praised be the Lord, our God, the Lord of all generations. You are holy: Awesome is your name. You are our Ruler and our Helper, our Savior and Protector.

Over and over again, it made me uneasy. Was that sucking up to God? I don't think God wants all that adoration. I believe God prefers you to do something good in life.

Tikkun olam is a Hebrew expression that means "fix the world." It is at the center of a Jewish mystical belief that the world was created broken, and it is up to us to fix it, in any way we can. At the same time, we must remember that "it is not up to us to complete the work, nor are we free to desist from it."

One of the ways to make this world a better place is to create beauty. I do that every Friday night as I welcome the Sabbath by praying over the candles in candlesticks left by my mother, which she brought over from Russia. They must be well over a hundred years old. In doing that, I am reminded of my mother, I feel closer to God, to my family, and I have increased The Light, even if only for a moment. You can pray in your own way.

I promised to be a "good boy." I believe God wants me to help others. And so I pray in my own way.

A medieval rabbi once explained prayer with a wonderful parable. When we pray, he said, we think we are changing God. Think of a man in a rowboat who is pulling himself to shore. To someone who does not know what is going on, it might appear that he is really pulling the shore closer to himself. Similarly, when we pray, it may appear that we are trying to pull God closer to us. But we are really pulling ourselves closer to God.

So my advice to everyone is: Pray, however you perceive that Higher Power to be. Pray, it will help you.

A few weeks after Yom Kippur, I was at the club having lunch. I felt someone's hand on my shoulder and a whisper in my ear.

"I decided to suck up to Him." I turned around. It was my friend Rick.

"Why?" I said.

"It wouldn't hurt." He smiled and walked away.

Seventeen.

Have Stroke,
Will Travel

For the first year following my stroke, I felt like a caterpillar, moving about slowly and clinging to my cocoon. Now I had learned enough to help me cope with my life—a "Manual" for survival. It was still hard for me to leave my cocoon, but I knew I must. I spent so much time in it because I felt safe. I certainly didn't travel far. I drove my car to the office, ten minutes, or to the doctor's office, eleven minutes, or to the golf course, twelve minutes. Now, in the second year after my stroke, I was going to test my wings and take off like a butterfly into the world.

My wife is an avid tennis player. The time was approaching for the Wimbledon games in London. Anne and I went there every year, before my stroke. Now I knew climbing those steps would be too difficult on my bad knees (boy, I have a lot of things wrong with me!). But that wasn't the only reason. I was frightened to make such a long trip. I didn't want to deprive her and I suggested she go alone. She refused to leave me.

I decided to be bold. "Anne, why don't you go to Wimbledon and I will meet you in London in a week." She looked at me in surprise. "We can fly to Israel to inaugurate the playgrounds we built in Jerusalem, then on to Jordan." Anne was astounded.

I had been sad to learn that King Hussein had died not long after I received his letter. I was surprised when King Abdullah, the son of Hussein, wished to fulfill his father's request. The invitation was still open. Anne and I had a deal.

I had great trepidation about taking such a long trip. But Anne was now in London and couldn't see my concern. A stroke obliterates your self-confidence. Every day you have a critical point when you think you will not be able to talk. At the end of each day, your speech really disintegrates. Of course that may have something to do with one or two stiff drinks. But I am willing to pay *that* price.

My strongest safety blanket is my wife. It's comforting to know that there is always someone to look after you. I feel better knowing she is in the next room. When we argue, I end it by saying, "If you ever leave me, I'm going with you."

One day, Anne read an article in the *Los Angeles Times* about the deplorable condition of all the playgrounds in the Los Angeles schools. She initiated a program to rehabilitate the dilapidated playgrounds. When a playground is finished, I accompany my wife to the inauguration. She has set up more than a hundred playgrounds. Now her plans are for four hundred more. I am very proud of what my wife has accomplished. Once I said to her, "Anne, this is a really great project, what can I do to help?" Her answer: "Make a movie . . . we need the money!"

I tried to hide my fears of taking such a long trip—a direct flight, L.A. to London, twelve hours. Forty thousand feet in the air, rushing toward my destination, all my lifelines severed. I tried to relax. I tried to sleep. Images of my mother and ice cream with my father didn't work at that altitude. But I prayed a lot.

I walked off the plane like a general. "Never let the troops see you sway," my son Joel always advises me.

"How was the trip?" my wife asked.

"I learned one thing."

"What's that?"

"Never take a sleeping pill and a laxative on the same night."

"What?"

"I'm kidding. I slept all the way."

She laughed, but I know she didn't believe me. It didn't matter, because in our embrace, I was holding my lifeline.

Eighteen.
Playgrounds
in Israel

When I play a strong character in a movie, I search for some weakness, and if I play a weak character, I search for some strength. Now I felt as if I had used up all of my strength dealing with my stroke. Now I could afford to be weak.

I have a confession: Since my stroke, I feel

like a little boy who clings to his mother's hand for security. I liked that feeling. What do you think of Spartacus now?

Our time in London passed quickly, and before I knew it, we had boarded a private plane, a Challenger, to fly us to Tel Aviv. This time I felt secure. I even let go of Anne's hand. We landed in Israel.

We dedicated two playgrounds in the Old City. The first was a large park for the Arab children, on a high plateau overlooking Jerusalem. There were many steps to climb and I couldn't make it with my bad knees. I arrived in a small motor cart, bouncing up the steps to the playground.

At the entrance I was pleased to see the inscription that I had insisted on: IN MEMORY OF THE OKLAHOMA CHILDREN. I wanted to remind people that when bombs fall, innocent children are

This moment was an unexpected honor for me and I cherish it. Now, I'm going back to school!

killed. Now I was playing soccer with happy Arab children. It did not escape me that they kicked

*The inaugurations of playgrounds are always happy events,
but I hate it when my wife wakes me up in the morning,
telling me that I "have to go to school."*

the ball very gently to me. I always hate those
reminders of my age. Anne raced around the

park on a scooter to applause. And when one of the children said, "Your daughter is very good on the scooter," I was tempted to kick the cute kid in the pants!

Land is very scarce in the Old City. The stone houses are perched one on top of the other or very close together, the cobblestone streets are no more than alleys, there are not many places for children to play. Sometimes they use rooftops, and dream of a soccer field. Not far away, we went to the Jewish quarter. The kids were dressed in uniforms to celebrate the opening of a new soccer field. A small boy, not tall enough to reach the microphone, recited a long poem that he had composed, ending with *"With thanks to Kirk who gave us this soccer field."* I was happy.

Nineteen.
Jordan! Jordan!

When I first heard of the death of King Hussein, I was devastated. His letter to me after my Oscar appearance filled me with such hope. And now I could never accept his invitation to "visit" in Jordan. I was wrong. His son, the new king, took over the invitation.

*   *   *

The next day of our trip, our driver, Ronin, drove us to the Allenby Bridge at the Israeli-Jordanian border. As we approached, I felt almost grateful for my stroke. It was bringing excitement to my life. For the first time, I was visiting Jordan and the king.

We flew first to Jerash to view what is perhaps the finest example of Roman ruins in the world. I was able to experience the work of talented artists who lived two thousand years ago. I stood in the center of the amphitheater, banks of seats in a semicircle arching around me. I spoke (with my speech impediment) and could be heard at the farthest seats. But I'm not sure that they could make out what I was saying.

That evening we dined at a restaurant carved out of an old stone stable in the capital city of Amman. It was very colorful, lively, and joyous. Children were dining with their parents and everyone was dancing. Anne surprised me by dancing with them. We gorged ourselves on Jordanian food and promptly went to bed. We were to meet with the king and queen in the morning.

The long roadway leading to the royal residence was interspersed with armed guards standing at attention. King Abdullah greeted us, casually attired, and the queen joined soon after. The queen is a beautiful young lady (a Palestinian from Kuwait) who speaks English perfectly; she had attended UCLA, and the king had been educated at Eaglebrook, the same school my son Michael attended. I was the only one struggling with the English language!

The king offered his private helicopter to take us to Petra. I gulped. How could I say that ever since my accident, helicopters frightened the hell

Kirk Douglas

With the king and queen in their residence in Jordan. What a nice couple.

out of me? I was always haunted by the two young fliers who were killed. Now I know I'm a good actor, because I concealed my anxiety.

With the royal helicopter, the trip took forty minutes. The noise inside the cabin made it difficult to talk. It was nice to just look.

From the air, you see tall, arid, sandstone mountains and a winding gorge with towering cliffs on each side. On the ground, you arrive at a narrow split where the cliffs almost meet, and through that crevice, you catch a glimpse of the magical city. Petra, one of the most unique places in the world, had been lost beneath the sands of the desert for hundreds of years.

A year ago, when the invitation from King Hussein arrived, I couldn't conceive of taking a trip to far-off Jordan and Petra. Now here I was— a "stroke of luck."

From the ground, the experience only grows. The first thing that meets your eyes is a beautiful edifice called the Monastery. You can't believe this was all created from a mountain of stone—tall Corinthian columns delicately carved on top. In the sunlight, the stone turns to a reddish pink. Imagine, this was all constructed over two thousand years ago. As you walk through the city of stone, the beauty of it is staggering.

Years ago, when Jordan and Israel were not so friendly, Israeli soldiers, as well as young adults,

Kirk Douglas

We are given a memento of our trip to that marvelous place—Petra.

crawled over the border just to get a glimpse of this magical city. It was considered a rite of passage. Many were killed by Jordanian snipers, and still they came. A beautiful Israeli ballad was composed about this enchanted city called Petra. How amazing to risk your life to see something beautiful. You have to be very young. The song was eventually banned because it only encouraged adventurous Israeli youths to risk death to see Petra.

My Stroke of Luck

I rode a camel. It was too difficult for me to walk. But have you ever ridden a camel? Avoid it if you can! I marveled at what these bedouin nomads had created. Many of them still live in dwellings carved in the hillside. These caves are cool in the heat of summer and warm in the cold winter.

It was time to leave this enchanted city. In the royal helicopter we made our way along the Jordan side of the Dead Sea, the lowest spot on earth. The captain's voice came through our headsets: "We are now flying below sea level." I was just beginning to wrap my mind around that concept when my reverie was interrupted. Our guide pointed to another mountaintop: "And that's Mount Nebo, where Moses stood and glimpsed the Promised Land he would never enter." I gasped and held my breath. It made me think of Martin Luther King Jr.'s speech: "I Have a Dream."

I looked over Mount Nebo in awe. Moses also had a speech impediment. Of all the characters in the Bible, Moses is my hero. What a life! Set adrift as a baby on the river Nile, rescued by an Egyptian princess and raised as a prince in the palace, fled the palace after killing an Egyptian he saw beating a Jew, married Zipporah, a woman not of the Jewish faith . . . and at the age of eighty, Moses hears the voice of God commanding him to lead the Jewish slaves out of Egypt. Then the story begins . . .

The voice of the guide continued through the headphones. "Moses died there, and no one knows where he's buried." I looked out at this wide span of mountains and deserts and wondered about the God that had taken away the soul of Moses with a kiss. I felt a little guilty flying quickly to Israel, the land that Moses only got a glimpse of after forty years of wandering.

Twenty.

A Bloody Nose
in Tel Aviv

In Tel Aviv, Anne and I dedicated a playground in honor of Yitzhak Rabin, the prime minister of Israel who went to Oslo in an attempt to make peace with Arafat and the Palestinians. When he returned to Israel, he was murdered by a Jew, a young right-wing student.

That evening we attended a concert conducted by our friend Zubin Mehta. Before the concert began, we went backstage to visit him. Zubin insisted that I say something to the audience. I tried to demur, but he was insistent. "Zubin, what can I say?"

He had a quick reply: "You can announce that our solo violinist cannot play tonight because he has chicken pox."

I agreed, and before going onstage, I asked the Israeli stage manager, what do you call chicken pox in Hebrew? He said, "It's called *avababout*." "What?" I asked, and he repeated it. *"A-va-ba-bout."* Then I walked onstage to a very warm reception and said: "I'm sorry, the solo violinist will not be able to perform tonight because he has *avababout*." Then I looked at the audience and said, "If you are wondering why I was chosen to make this announcement"—all this with my slurred speech—"it's because I can pronounce *a-va-ba-bout*." I went offstage to gales of laughter.

After the concert, we had supper with Zubin Mehta at a friend's apartment in Tel Aviv. Shimon Peres sat at one end of the table, Ariel Sharon at the other end. The sharp exchanges were fascinating. This was shortly before all hell broke out in Israel.

That night in bed, I relived this wonderful evening. I still heard the laughter, the applause, and the scintillating conversation. I had forgotten about my stroke. In the middle of the night, I was awakened. I turned on the light. The pillow was drenched with blood gushing from my nose. I couldn't stop the flow. The Coumadin that I was taking acts as a blood thinner. Any cut gushes blood.

Is this it? I wondered. What a way to go—with a bloody nose! I felt foolish, but the blood kept dripping through the cotton I stuffed up my nose.

I could see the headline now. DOUGLAS DIES FROM A BLOODY NOSE. I joke about death, but I think about it often—seriously. I look at the obituary page every day. Yesterday was a bad day. Most people who were written up died at eighty-four, my age, or younger. I don't like to see that. I feel better when I read about people dying at age ninety or more!

Anne put in a call to my doctor in Los Angeles—five thousand miles to discuss a bloody nose. The formula was ice and pressure. The flow finally stopped. Blood was all over the towels, pillows, and sheets. It was a bloody reminder of my stroke.

Twenty-One.
Berlin

When we reached the airport for our flight
home, there was no motorcar waiting to take me to
the plane, only a wheelchair. I was embarrassed,
but I got in and never looked up as Anne wheeled
me like a cripple to the plane.

Now we were on our way, with a stop in Berlin
to pick up a Lifetime Achievement award at the
Berlin Film Festival. I must have at least fifteen

Kirk Douglas

Lifetime Achievement awards. When my son Michael received a Lifetime Achievement award, I felt like I was ready to receive an "After-Lifetime Achievement" award.

A bevy of photographers and journalists greeted me in Berlin. In broken English, they were peppering me with questions. One journalist spoke up in a loud voice. "As a Jew, how does it affect you to be in Berlin?" There was a momentary silence in which a montage of pictures raced through my mind. *Shattering glass, "Heil Hitler" salutes, Jews being herded into freight cars, piles of emaciated Jews, ovens, dark smoke coming out of chimneys.*

They were waiting for my answer. This is what I said: "The last century has been a disaster. My generation did not do a good job—so many wars— so much killing—and of course here in Germany, the Holocaust, perhaps the worst crime of all—the

attempt to annihilate a race as a final solution."
They were all listening. . . .

"But I don't think children should be pun-
ished for the sins of their fathers. We should all
hope that this millennium will see better people.
We should do all we can to give our children that
chance."

"So, why did you come back to Berlin?"

I ignored the reporter who asked this question,
but his words bothered me. I didn't know of a
proper reason for a Jew to stay in Berlin.

That night I was presented with the Golden
Bear at the Berlin Film Festival. The presentation
was made in English. It made an impact when I
gave my acceptance speech in German. I think the
German language sounds better with a stroke.

That same night we had a wonderful Wiener
schnitzel with some friends and a Jewish lady who
lived in Berlin throughout the war. She was such a

happy person, smiling and laughing. But when I was told that her whole family—her parents, her grandmother, aunts, uncles, and cousins—perished in different concentration camps, I blurted out the question "So why do you stay in Berlin?"

She was still smiling as she gave me this answer: "I owe that to the 'Little Heroes.'"

"I don't understand," I said. With a sigh, she came over and sat closer to me.

"When the Gestapo came to get them, my parents sent me to a little hotel to save my life. The owner was the first Little Hero. She kept me safe for a couple of nights. When it became dangerous, I met my second Little Hero. Or, should I say Heroine? She was our former housekeeper. She hid me for a while and endangered her own life. Then I lived in a cloister. My Little Heroes were the nuns who took care of me when I was very sick. They never asked questions. When the situation became dangerous, my next Little Hero was a policeman, who didn't agree with the Nazis. All through the war, I was lucky to find Little Heroes that helped me until the Russians came in."

"So, why do you stay here?" I asked again. She looked at me and sighed. "I thought about it, but I feel I owe it to the Little Heroes that helped me. Not everyone here was wicked."

Her story impressed me so much that when I came home, I wrote an op-ed piece for the *New York Times* about my meeting with Inge. I understood why she chose to remain in Berlin. We are always looking for a hero to emulate and to lead us. Very often our leaders fall short and topple with clay feet. We must reach for the Little Heroes in life—and try to be one ourselves.

It's not hard to be a Little Hero. You aren't obligated to save a life—but you are obligated to try to help other people. Follow my "Operator's Manual," and perhaps if you are lucky, you, too, might become a Little Hero. Shortly after my op-

ed piece was printed in the *New York Times,* I got a
letter from the mayor of Berlin, Eberhard Diepgen.
He asked my permission to translate and publish
my article in Germany. I gave him permission.

Twenty-Two.

Going Home,
Going Home

When I returned from my travels, I entered my room and stretched out on the bed, my little safety net during the early days after my stroke. This is where it all happened. There was the chair that I sat in when I felt the thin line trace across my cheek. This is the room where I did so many oral aerobics. It was here that I devised an Operator's Manual, which enabled me to go out into the world again.

As I lay on my bed, Danny and Foxy jumped up and started licking at me. They were glad to see me. I was happy. My stroke had led me on a great adventure and changed me into a different person—a person whom I like.

Happiness is a temporary state. Waves of depression continue to ebb and flow, a relentless tide, no matter how hard I strive to subdue them. I have learned to live with uncertainty, to know that in life, there are no guarantees. I have learned that no matter how much you believe your house to be a safe haven, a fortress against the dangers of living, the hand of fate can pass through to touch you lightly on the shoulder, to smite you or your loved ones, to draw, with a sharp pointed line, on your cheek, from your temple to your chin.

My Stroke of Luck

When you feel too weak to carry your burden, look to the actions of other human beings for inspiration. Embedded in my mind is the Seattle Special Olympics of a few years ago. A story was told to me about nine contestants, all physically or mentally disabled, assembled at the starting line for the hundred-yard dash.

At the gun, they all started out, not exactly in a dash, but with a relish for running the race to the finish and winning. All, that is, except one little boy, who stumbled on the asphalt, tumbled over a couple of times, and began to cry.

The other eight heard the boy cry. They slowed down and looked back. Then they all turned around and went back . . . every one of them.

One girl with Down's syndrome bent down and kissed him and said, "This will make it better." Then all nine linked arms and walked together to the finish line. Everyone in the stadium stood, and the cheering went on for several minutes. People who were there are still telling the story.

Why? Because deep down we know that what matters in this life is more than winning for ourselves. What matters in this life is helping others win, even if it means slowing down and changing our course. We all want happiness. Life teaches us that we achieve happiness when we seek the happiness and well-being of others.

I started writing this book to try and help people understand a stroke, and find a way to deal with it and function in life. I wanted to construct an Operator's Manual that would be a guide for recovering from a stroke. My stroke taught me so much, and for all that it stole, it gave me even more. In the process of healing, my life has changed for the better. Now I want to share what I have learned.

But in looking over my Operator's Manual, I

had an epiphany. Dealing with a stroke, dealing with any ailment or misfortune, is no different from the way we all should live our lives.

My Operator's Manual

1. When things go bad, always remember it could be worse.

2. Never, never give up. Keep working on your speech and on your life.

3. Never lose your sense of humor. Laugh at yourself, laugh with others.

4. Stem depression by thinking of, reaching out to, and helping others. Strive to be a Little Hero.

5. Do unto others as you would have them do unto you.

6. Pray. Not for God to cure you, but to help you help yourself.

Helen Keller, blind and deaf from birth, said, "When we do the best we can, we never know what miracle is wrought in our life, or the life of another."

We all have a handicap—big or small. But we must overcome our hardships to become better people. We must try, we must try.